THE GLASGOW

The Glasgow Wheelers

A Scottish cycling history

KENNY PRYDE

Biscuit Tin Media

Copyright © Kenny Pryde 2023

The Author asserts the moral right to
be identified as the author of this work.

ISBN 978-1-915972-16-3

Published by Biscuit Tim Media with YouCaxton Publications 2023

All rights reserved. No part of this publication may be reproduced, stored in a retrieval system, or transmitted in any form or by any means, electronic, mechanical, photocopying, recording or otherwise, without the prior permission of the author.

This book is sold subject to the condition that it shall not, by way of trade or otherwise, be lent, resold, hired out or otherwise circulated without the author's prior consent in any form of binding or cover other than that in which it is published and without a similar condition including this condition being imposed on the subsequent purchaser.

YouCaxton Publications
www.youcaxton.co.uk

Contents

PROLOGUE ix
1. *IN THE BEGINNING* 1
2. *WHICH SIDE ARE YOU ON?* 15
3. *CHANGING GEARS* 34
4. *CRAWLING FROM THE WRECKAGE* 49
5. *GLASGOW'S SWINGING SIXTIES* 81
6. *BIG TIME CHARLIES* 96
7. *TO THE CENTRE OF THE CITY* 119
8. *THE MILLENNIUM BLUES* 139
Thanks and acknowledgments 157
Index 158

I couldn't have done it without Sandra and Katie.
Dream team.

PROLOGUE

HAVE YOU NOTICED? Centenaries are ten a penny these days. It's an inescapable fact that the older you become, the more centenaries you get to see, the more the clock ticks over, the older everything around us gets. Something or someone is claiming some kind of anniversary every day. Queen Elizabeth was writing so many 100th birthday telegrams to her ageing subjects its rumoured she had sub-contracted the job to Serco in her later years.

On the other hand, in 2023, there weren't too many cycling clubs that could claim to be a hundred years old, which helped make the argument for writing this book. Additionally there are those who claim that the Glasgow Wheelers is the oldest continuously existing cycling club in Scotland. That may or may not be true – feel free to go away and argue among yourselves – but that detail adds something to a hundred years of history too. In the end though, I'd argue that its not the centenary of the club or its claim to be the oldest in Scotland that makes this book a worthwhile enterprise.

It's the fact that throughout its history, various members of the Glasgow Wheelers were wrapped up in the development of British cycling – of world cycling even – and several who passed through the club were key players in Scottish cycling history. Plus, there are some great stories of races won and lost, dirty deeds and noble gestures, most of which deserve to be recorded, even if some would prefer them to be forgotten.

So, by way of commemorating the centenary of the foundation of the Glasgow Wheelers, this book will attempt the impossible. Which is to say, the following chapters will try to weave together the history of the club with the development of competitive cycling in Scotland and the influence of its members in Britain and beyond. From its origins in the early years of the 20th century bike craze through the tumult of two world wars and organisational intrigues, across periods of boom and slump, the Glasgow Wheelers Cycling Club has never been far from the action.

The history of the Glasgow Wheelers in some ways mirrors that of cycling in Scotland itself. It deserves to be recorded for posterity, and those members who played only minor parts in cycling history are worthy of some recognition.

Inevitably a historical undertaking like this is doomed to be incomplete, to be partial, biased and fuzzy at the edges. There will be errors and omissions and perhaps people missing entirely, for which, apologies in advance. For those who feel hard done by hopefully the next historian will be able to fill the gaps and right some perceived sporting injustices.

1

IN THE BEGINNING

THE BRITISH BROADCASTING Corporation was formed in 1923, the same year as the Glasgow Wheelers. Like the Wheelers, the newly created BBC was headed by a Scotsman, Managing director John Reith. Unlike fellow centenarian the BBC, there's precious little information on the Wheelers earliest days.

All joking aside, given that no actual documents with eye-witness statements of the event exist, the best we can say is that the Glasgow Wheelers was formed in 1923. The Wheelers 'was' formed, rather than the Glasgow Wheelers 'were' formed because, of course, the Glasgow Wheelers is *a* club, a singular entity. After all, there's only one Glasgow Wheelers, but where did it emerge from?

Accustomed as we now are to finding everything we want online, there is – alas – no digital archive that details the formation of the Wheelers and, given that a hundred years have passed, those involved are no longer with us. So, bearing all that in mind, all we can confidently state is that the current incarnation of the Glasgow Wheelers dates from 1923. And even with that 'fact,' there's a tiny grain of doubt, because we can't ignore a story that suggests there was, in fact, another even older version of the club. Unsurprisingly, there's no written or digital archive of that entity either.

Which means there's no hard evidence of a 'Glasgow Wheelers' that may have been active from around the turn of the century, though a thesis buried in Stirling University titled 'The development of sport in Glasgow, 1850-1914' mentions the existence of a Glasgow

Wheelers cycling club as "formed by riders in the Townhead area during 1904."

The reference in the thesis for this curious historical nugget was given as the Glasgow *Evening Times* of the era, which is where the evidence trail goes cold. More than this, there is nothing, though if its accurate, the name, if nothing else, was the same. What that muddy story does illustrate though is that cycling was a popular pastime well before the invention of derailleur gears...

The earliest histories of many cycling clubs around the turn of the 19th and 20th Century are muddied because – remarkably – there had been over a hundred cycling clubs in Scotland in the final twenty-five years of the 19th Century. Perhaps surprisingly, cycling had been a popular fad in the 1880s and there are solid records of no fewer than 59 cycling clubs in Glasgow in 1898, most of which were affiliated to the National Cyclists Union in London.

The records of the Scottish Cyclists' Union insist that the organisation was actually 'Founded in 1889 and reconstituted in 1952' which is evidence of some level of organisation among cyclists, even if almost no details remain from that first period. In any case, that very likely means that some of Scotland's oldest clubs shared a name with earlier incarnations of those prehistoric organisations, if not the spirit, sport or machinery.

It turns out that for the final two decades of the 19th Century cycling was the trendy thing to do among the middle-classes who formed clubs and organised runs during a 'season' that lasted from April to October. Those first clubs would organise rides – or 'excursions' as they were known – meeting at Anniesland Toll, Charing Cross or Ibrox stadium before heading out to Bridge of Weir, Erskine Ferry, Strathblane and Busby, all kitted out in club colours.

In fact some of those clubs were organising time trials and road races on the open roads too, albeit that the races were 10 miles long. Thus, on the south side of Glasgow, the Langside Bicycle club had 27 members in 1894 and a calendar of club runs was published at the start of every season.

Existing club records note that on Thursday 5 April 1894 the members met at Langside Academy and rode down to Fenwick to inaugurate another season which was due to finish on 27 September with another jaunt south west to Fenwick. In between, there were rides to Beith, Balloch, Hamilton, Strathaven, Bridge of Weir and Crossford. Calendar days were marked off for five-mile club handicap races however, as well as national 'Bicycle meets' in Edinburgh.

Perhaps surprisingly, given the basic nature of bikes and components, there were debates about technical specifications even then. The Langside club records of 1894 note that it was proposed that "the *minimum* weight of machine to be ridden at Championships and Handicaps races be 40 pounds." An amendment proposing the minimum weight should be reduced to a mere 35 pounds was rejected by 13 votes to five. Suddenly the ride up any hill – on a single-speed bike tipping the scales at at least 40 pounds (or 18kg if you prefer) – starts to look like much more of a challenge.

That earliest cycling fad didn't last though, and by 1910 there were 'only' 27 clubs left in Glasgow and the focus was still on Saturday rides into the countryside rather than competition. For many in the Edwardian era, the ownership of a Rudge, Swift or Elswick was today's equivalent of a German-made SUV (with a bike rack, of course), a form of conspicuous consumption.

However, cycling clubs began to lose their 'flash' appeal when the price of bikes started to fall. This meant that the lower orders took to two wheels, obliging wealthier Glaswegians to shift onto four wheels if they wanted to display their superior social status with the latest trendy big-ticket toy.

The bursting of the cycling bubble left bikes in the hands of a more blue-collar demographic and a shift away from 'excursions' towards a more competitive activity, at which point the dandy in cashmere and silk was replaced by a more utilitarian rider, who had more interest in racing and prize money than the 'gentleman' who had been out to impress the locals and the ladies.

Inevitably, wherever there are two people on bikes, there will always be an element of competition and, even if the focus of the earlier clubs was on social riding, there were already competitive events. According to Wheelers historian John Thayne, track racing star R. A. 'Bobby' Vogt was a member of that earlier version of the Wheelers, as well as being the club president.

There's no club record of this, though Vogt certainly competed for Clydesdale Harriers on two wheels as early as 1893. Vogt was born in Glasgow on 15 February 1869 and took to racing on a high-wheeled 'Ordinary' (think of a Penny Farthing style) in 1888 before switching to the newer and more conventional 'Safety' diamond-framed bikes in 1886. The arrival of the Safety frame design coincided, within a few years, with Ayrshire-born William Boyd Dunlop's new pneumatic tyre, in 1888.

Dunlop got an Irish bicycle maker named Edlin to turn out a pair of rims and then asked Edinburgh company, Thornton's, to make pneumatic tyres. The tyres were constructed from lightweight Arbroath sail canvas coated in India rubber and, needless to say, were a revelation in terms of comfort and speed. It was also reported that those prototype tyres did 3,000 miles and suffered no punctures. Imagine – 3,000 miles without a puncture!

Around the same time, Vogt raced in track meetings that were part of sports days – athletics, five-a-side football and cycling – held on cinder tracks around football grounds at Ibrox, Hampden, Barrowfield and Parkhead, attended by up to 14,000 paying spectators. Indeed, the 1897 World track championships – with professional and amateur events – were held at Celtic's Parkhead stadium, albeit on a specially built banked concrete track.

According to an August 1891 newspaper cutting, "R.A. Vogt is a special favourite with the Celtic crowd and it is their sincere wish that Bobbie will soon again be permitted to lead the way in Scottish cycling as he has done for the past few years, and that he may yet obtain one of the English championships. The victory of Vogt in the half-mile scratch race at Parkhead stadium sent the crowd into fits of delight." Difficult as they may be to envisage, these track meets were essentially pro-am events, with serious prize money on offer, so regulations concerning professional riders were controversial. There was under-the-table appearance money with generous travel expenses on offer and where there's pro racing, there's always betting.

It's worth noting too that with paying crowds of several thousand there was money to be made and richer promoters, including those at Parkhead, started to invite 'foreigners' to generate interest in a sport that was also on the wane by 1910. Their popular demise was down to less well-off clubs not being able to afford the fees for foreign professionals which meant they ran more locally-focussed events. However when those 'local races for local people' failed to attract crowds, the events petered out, being no longer considered worth the effort of organising.

This, then, was the background cycling culture that the Glasgow Wheelers was resurrected into in 1923, the 'Vogt version' having vanished, like many others, around the time of world war one. In the early 1920s, the Scottish racing scene featured well-attended track meets, time trials and no (officially) organised open road races, all of which were overseen by the Scottish Amateur Racing Association (SARA), a loose assembly formed in 1889.

As relatively close as the era might seem – recognisable club names, track racing meetings and familiar race formats – the landscape of work and culture of 1920s Scotland manages to be simultaneously familiar yet strange. Searching through 1920s archives, the geography and street names, the roads, hills and villages of the West of Scotland are all recognisable, but when examined more closely, they're slightly alien. The 1923 towns with their church steeple landmarks are all already there in those early maps. Even in the 1920s Drymen and Aberfoyle were popular cycling destinations, but the housing is primitive, while the suburban sprawl, the council housing estates and high rise flats are totally absent, nowhere to be seen. The routes and road numbers are the same, (thus, for example, A81 is still the A81) but they are often cobbled or unmade, horses and carts are familiar sights, while cars are still a rarity. The 1920s trains are steam-driven, the coal that powers both them and the factories of Glasgow – still proudly the second city of Empire – are decidedly not 'smokeless.' It's still Glasgow, but not *quite* as we know it.

Funnily enough the bikes of the 1920s looked a bit different too.

The cycling resurgence in the early decades of the 20th century had been principally driven by the emergence of the 'Safety bicycle' design in 1886 which effectively standardised the 'diamond' frame still ridden a century later. Prior to this, bikes we would call 'Penny Farthings' dominated, but the 'Safety' design was a proverbial game changer. With wheels of equal size, rubber tyres, spoked wheels, a front brake, chain and sprocket – the machine refined by John Kemp Starley in Coventry was a 'bike' we would all still recognise and be able to ride.

When Dunlop (or might we controversially ask if it was fellow Scot Robert Thomson?) developed the pneumatic tyre in 1888, we were up and all running more smoothly over Glasgow cobbles. Bike manufacturers and frame builders increased in number to cope with the upswing in interest and even if the frame geometry and fork rakes look strange, they're not so far removed from many modern bike shapes.

Has anyone still got a Glasgow-built 'New Howe' dating from 1895 in their shed? Perhaps a Hampden Cycle Company frame? Probably not, because although there were a few Scottish bike manufacturers in the 1920s, most bikes still came from the Midlands of England from Raleigh, BSA, Dawes, Saxon and Hercules factories. Honourable and inevitable mention must be made here of David Rattray and his sister Agnes who opened their first bike shop in Townhead, in 1900. Glasgow Wheeler Rattray would, in due course, produce 'Flying Scot' racing and touring frames, one of the few Scottish bespoke builders to have lasted into the post-world war two period and into the 1970s.

If it's hard to imagine what Scotland's roads were like a century ago both in terms of their condition and the other road users, it's a safe bet 21st Century riders would notice some differences. We would be at less risk from motorised traffic for one, though anyone who believes that the 'gravel riding' craze that emerged in the 2010s was a new hybrid of Tarmac and dirt would feel perfectly at home on Scotland's back roads of the period.

The Glasgow – indeed Scotland – of the 1920s was different in that there were only 380,000 vehicles in the *whole* of the UK. By 2015, DVLA registration figures reveal that Scottish roads alone were 'home' to three *million* cars. Back when the first Glasgow Wheelers club run was organised, car ownership was still limited to the upper middle classes and those early years must have been traffic-free bliss, even if it didn't last, as car sales began to increase. It had grown so much so that in 1920 the Roads Act required local Councils to register all vehicles and give them a registration number. Prior to that, if you had been wiped out by a Sunday driver, they didn't even have a number plate to report.

If there weren't as many cars and delivery vans on Glasgow roads when the 'new' 1923 Wheelers was formed, then it was at a time when the population of Glasgow was just over one million souls. Thus far (by 2023) that has turned out to be Glasgow's peak as its populations escaped to the ever-expanding suburbs – working hard to live up to its second city of Empire tag. Given the national census of 1911 had the entire population of Scotland pegged at 4,760,904 it's safe to say that Glasgow was a major centre of social, economic and sporting activity.

While it's relatively easy to give broad brush context to the Glasgow of the 1920s, details elude us when trying to put flesh on the bones of the early years of the Glasgow Wheelers. It's not like the Wheelers are unique in this 'lost in the mists of time' scenario, given that no Scottish time trial records exist, at all, since nobody thought to collate them till 1931! In the end, all that can be said with any degree of certainty is that the club was formed when a half a dozen riders from the Douglas Cycling Club – based in the coal mining heartlands of north Lanarkshire – broke away to form the 'new' Wheelers. The names of those early founder members are essentially all that remains: Tommy Crawford, Fred Brookes, Hugh Cassels, Andy Malcolm and Italian-born Valentin 'Val' Del Vecchio.

The story goes that this group quit the Douglas over the allocation of prize money. Its also possible that the growth in popularity of cycling after the Great War was such that a new club, based nearer the city, was called for. That first season, 1923-24, the Glasgow Wheelers comprised 37 riders, all paying five shillings (25 pence) subs and most of them forking out another 3/6 for a cloth badge.

In any case, speculation aside, of that initial group, Del Vecchio was the star performer and the one with a highly unusual back story. Del Vecchio had in fact been born in Venafro, in the province of Isernia, about 100 miles south east of Rome. No sooner had Del Vecchio been born in 1898 than his parents emigrated to Glasgow, setting up a hair dressers in Shettleston. Del Vecchio and his older brother David started riding as teenagers, often heading out to Aberfoyle and getting involved, latching on to the back of club runs and mixing it in the inevitable 'habble' finale. A competitive character, Del Vecchio started to train and take things more seriously to the point at which he became one of the best riders in Scotland, his main claim to fame being that he was the first rider in Britain to break two hours for a straight-out 50 mile time trial – a 1-55 is the only time we have any record of – set on a fixed wheel bike with no brakes in the 1930s. For the sake of historical accuracy, it should be noted that Del Vecchio set this mark when he was a member of the Douglas CC, but we can't hold that against him. In a curious twist, Val's son Ernie, riding for the Glasgow Suburban CC, would go on to post the first sub-two hour '50' on a recognised out-and-back course in Scotland, a 1-59-51 in 1954. In fact Ernie 'E.V.' Mitchell was a formidable short and middle distance time triallist, setting records at 25 and 50 miles in the mid 1950s. That was a few years further down the road, by which time the family name had changed from Del Vecchio to Mitchell on account of the anti-Italian sentiment that boiled up during world war two. We digress for the first, but not the last time...

Given the new cycling boom of the 1920s, its not a surprise to discover that a number of strong clubs formed or expanded in Glasgow and further afield during the 1920s. They included the Ivy, the Chryston Wheelers, the aforementioned Douglas as well as the Scottish Nomads, the Edinburgh Vulcan to back up the even older (1874!) Edinburgh Amateur BC. The Socialist-inspired National Clarion (formed in 1895 with its motto 'Fellowship is life') was meeting up in Govan from 1905 onwards, the Catholic St Christopher's arrived in 1938, the mostly Catholic Stella Maris, the Glasgow Merchants CC and the Glasgow Corporation Transport CC were all already part of the growing bike scene too. In due course, inspired by the 1922 formation of the women-only Rosslyn CC in London, Dundee would see the formation of its own women's club, the Heatherbell Ladies CC in 1929, beside the venerable Dundee Thistle CC, formed that same year.

It seems that in the early decades of the Twentieth century there was growth in what could be called 'outdoor' pursuits. In parallel with the cycling, the lure of the countryside – escaping the soot-caked cities still dominated by heavy industries and factory production – was increasingly attractive in the early years of the 20th Century. The Scottish Mountaineering Club had been formed in 1889, and the Ramblers Association in 1935, while the Scottish branch of the Youth Hostel Association also 'took off' after its formation in 1931. The SHYA provided cheap, clean accommodation for bike riders of the era and, at its peak in the early 1960s, there were 99 hostels in Scotland. Up till the 1980s hostelling trips were a staple part of most club riders year. At some point in the season, you were going to strap a Carradice saddle bag to your racing bike because it was likely the only bike you had.

It's something that will be hard to grasp for many modern readers, but in the 1920s and 1930s, when car ownership was very rare, the bike really *did* offer the individual mobility and a feeling of speed, escape and independence that was not easily found in daily life. In those decades cycling gave a sense of freedom that the modern rider has, inescapably, lost touch with.

It was not as if racing bikes were cheap and for the labourers, miners, shipbuilders and office workers who took part – they needed to commit to 'the bike.' In the 1920s a steel-framed roadster – not even a lightweight top-end race bike – from the likes of Raleigh would set you back £15, which sounds like a bargain. However, to give some financial context, in the pre-world war one years, a Glasgow labourer might earn 22 shillings a week, just over one pound, while a Scottish miner would earn 10 shillings seven pence per shift. In modern terms that's a total of 53 pence for a day's labour down a coal mine, in an industry where, in Lanarkshire collieries alone, 13 miners died in 1915, some as young as 15-years-old. Dirty, dangerous, badly paid and a hotbed for some ferocious sporting competitors, eager to escape the grime. In fact in 1923, the year of the club's emergence, 40 miners died when a pit flooded near Falkirk.

The testimony of a Tyneside miner from South Shields recorded in 1925, is one that many riders from Glasgow and Lanarkshire would no doubt understand. Having saved for years, the 29-year-old Tommy Turnbull went to Newcastle to spend his £8 on a bike and took his time about it. As reported by Neil Carter in his book *'Cycling and the British'* he records Turnbull saying that he "wouldn't be rushed" because he had "waited years and years for this and I wasn't going to buy anything until I was certain…It was only going to happen once." Turnbull and his new bike promptly joined the Tyne Dock Belle Vue CC and explained "for those like me who sometimes worked a sixteen-hour stretch in a dark and bad atmosphere and then went home to the smells of bone yards, factory smoke and the stink of the Tyne…in the countryside the air would be cool and fresh…on a bike you felt as though you were part of the countryside. Every week as soon as I saw the first green field I'd be breathing in and out as deeply as I could. I'd be striving to get rid of all the dust and muck from every part of my insides."

For those South Shields coalfields, you could substitute the pit heads of North Lanarkshire, for the Tyne, it could be the Clyde. The point here, really, is that the population was poorer and, you have to suspect, rather more robust. It's no surprise that cycling's long identification as a blue-collar sport is linked to its emergence from this culture.

Noted British historian Eric Hobsbawm was on to something when he wrote: "If physical mobility is an essential condition of freedom, the bicycle has probably been the greatest single device for achieving what Marx has called the full realisation of being human invented since Gutenberg, and the only one without obvious drawbacks." You have to wonder if the workers pedalling to their shifts at the pithead in Muirhead or to Denny's shipyards in Govan felt they were being 'fully realised,' but Hobsbawm certainly captures something of the joy of pushing on pedals and leaving the world of work behind.

However, there are some things that you can't escape, no matter how hard or how far you pedal. The Glasgow Wheelers emerged into an economically challenging environment after world war one, so its no shock to learn that emigration from Scotland peaked around this time too. Around 10 per cent of the population of Scotland packed up and headed for Canada, Australia, New Zealand, South Africa and the USA. Times were tough. In the same year the Wheelers was formed, Clydeside was badly hit. In 1922, the global Washington Naval treaty agreement to reduce the size of naval fleets had a terrible knock-on impact on Clyde shipbuilding and its local supply chains – guns, armour plate, mountings and ordinance production. The three biggest Glasgow yards laid off *18,000* shipbuilders. When merchant shipping came to a standstill after the Great Depression bit a few years later, the effect on the already struggling yards was catastrophic. It was enough to make anyone get on their bike and hit the road – assuming they could afford it. The thin silver lining to this economic cloud was that some laid-off engineers opened up bike shops and frame-building businesses. As ever, when things got bad, there was always sport to take your mind off things. Football was already well-established as Glasgow's sport of choice, but the first generation of Glasgow Wheelers could always scan the small print of newspapers to discover who and what was happening in European cycle sport.

When the Wheelers and other sporting-minded riders were discussing continental road racing in 1923, they would have known that a Frenchman named Henri Pelissier had won the seventeenth edition of the Tour de France, although it was a Tour format that few would recognise today.

The 1923 Tour was 5,386km long (current Grand Tours average 3,400km) in only 15 stages with no rest days. Given the distance and duration its not surprising that of 139 starters only 48 made it back to Paris with the *lantern rouge*, Frenchman Daniel Masson, over 48 hours down on Pelissier. Today's Tour takes around 80-something hours to complete, while Pelissier had to put in 222 hours in the saddle to complete his winning 'Grande Boucle' of France. Second place went to Ottavio Bottecchia, who would go on to win the following year and – much later – an American would ride a bike with his name on it to victory into Paris in 1989. The third place on the podium, occupied by Romain Bellenger, was over an hour down on Pelissier. The time gaps were different back then...

In 1923 the longest stage, between Les Sables d'Olonne on France's Atlantic coast and Bayonne, in the foothills of the Pyrenees, was 482 kilometres long. Stage winner Robert Jacquinot's time was just over 20 hours. The next leg was a mere 326 kilometres through the Pyrenees between Bayonne and Luchon, taking in the famous cols of the Aubisque, Tourmalet, Aspin and Peyresourde, none of which were even paved at the time.

Recall too that the riders only had two gears, one on each side of their rear wheels which meant they had to stop to flip the rear wheel to change. Effectively they had one gear for climbing and one for descending, though this year the riders were allowed to repair their bikes using spare parts, rather than having to find a friendly blacksmith.

A Tour route that was twice as long as it is today, epic stages, night riding, unmade mountain passes, minimal outside assistance, bikes with only two gears and so many drop outs, mechanicals and abandons that meant sometimes as few as 24 riders made it the finish line. These were the features of the Tour de France – and the Giro d'Italia – in the early 1920s.

Apart from the Tour and the Giro, many other races in the modern World Tour calendar already existed, well before the formation of the Glasgow Wheelers. Even if road racing was effectively banned in Scotland and the rest of the UK, it was already a fixture in cycling's continental European heartlands. Milan-San Remo (1907), Paris-Roubaix (1896), the Tour of Flanders (1913), Liege-Bastogne-Liege (1894) and the Tour of Lombardy (1905) were all already firmly in place, part of cycling's bedrock and rich mythology. The two Grand Tours – the Tour and the Giro – dated from 1903 and 1909 respectively, though they more resembled epic self-supported multi-day gravel events than modern stage races.

We can only speculate that Tommy Crawford, Fred Brookes, Hugh Cassels, Andy Malcolm and Val Del Vecchio, those new Glasgow Wheelers, might have been inspired by reports from France, Italy and Belgium. It's possible too that they might have read the results in '*Cycling*' magazine – founded in 1891 – the title that would, in time, become '*Cycling Weekly*' and for decades stand as the journal of record for Britain's club cyclists.

As the Wheelers became established in the 1920s, one name that needs to be added to the rebel quartet who founded the club. Pat McCabe, who joined in 1930, was a formidable track performer and the epitome of a club stalwart. McCabe was adept on grass and cinder tracks throughout the 1930s, racing in Ireland too. At one point, he held every Scottish track record from the quarter mile to three miles, pushed on by another early Wheelers track racing legend Willie Tagg. With the outbreak of the second world war McCabe joined the navy as a chief petty officer and, after demob, effectively hung up his racing wheels, though he was still active in the club half a century later, the epitome of the keen clubman which he remained until his death in 1993, aged 86.

Then, as former chairman and early club historian John Thayne noted, "About 1929 a most fortunate happening for the club was the entry of Jack Potter, a 100 mile time trial record holder at one point." It is to Potter that the Glasgow Wheelers 'owe' the long presence of the Thayne clan who were family friends of Potter and followed him to the club, with the arrival of a certain 'W. Thane' (sic) recorded in 1932. Like McCabe, Potter stayed for the long haul – he was still Honorary vice president 70 years later, while the Thayne family were still doing sterling work for the Wheelers and Scottish cycling too.

By the end of the roaring Twenties, the Glasgow Wheelers were all up and most of them were racing. In the mid 1930s, as Europe geared up for another war, the Wheelers grew and its membership roll call included David Rattray, Jimmy Brinkins, Jackie and Tommy Potter, and, in 1936, Donald Morrison and Alec Bilsland, the latter's sons were to have a significant role in Scottish cycling.

Alas, at this long interval, all we have left are some dog-eared black and white photos, as faded as the memories. But those names – Tommy Crawford, Fred Brookes, Hugh Cassels, Andy Malcolm, Val Del Vecchio, Pat McCabe, Jim Wallace, Jack Potter, Willie Tagg and John Stewart all played their part in growing the Wheelers in those early years. They all wrote, if not pages, then a few crucial lines in the founding of Glasgow's oldest and most famous club.

2

WHICH SIDE ARE YOU ON?

AFTER THE PRIVATIONS of the first world war and subsequent Great Depression, the 1930s had seen an increase in cycling activity of all kinds. The Glasgow Wheelers wasn't the only cycling club to have formed in the tumultuous 1920s and, as the 1930s arrived, the Scottish cycling scene grew rapidly. However, as new clubs emerged and memberships expanded, so too did the need for organisation. Between the wars, cyclists were getting *busy*. In Scotland's central belt, the Law Wheelers (1935) and then the Glasgow Eastern CC formed when it broke away from the Chryston Wheelers. We also saw the arrival of the Glasgow Ivy (1923), the Johnstone Wheelers (1926), Glasgow Nightingale (1925) the Regent CC (1933) and in 1941 the Glenmarnock was formed (by riders from the Ruther*glen* Nomads CC and Dal*marnock*). Out towards the west, the Lomond Roads CC arrived in 1933, while in north Lanarkshire, in Larkhall, the Royal Albert CC – with records dating back to 1901 – was restarted in 1926. Those clubs would, collectively, form the bedrock of cycling in the west of Scotland for decades to come.

While we scratch our heads trying to imagine the roads and bikes of the pre-WWII period, we would also struggle to recognise the organisations which controlled the nascent sport. In the 1920s and 1930s there was no Scottish Cycling and no British Cycling either. Rather there were competing organisations which all sought to curry favour with clubs, riders, as well as local and national governments – all the while keeping an eye on international sporting developments.

The cycling scene, both nationally and internationally, was a mess, in organisational terms at least.

In 1923, the year of the Wheelers formation, the London-based National Cyclists Union (NCU), was nominally in charge of UK cycle sport, an organisation that could trace its origins back to the 1880s. A rival, though in reality a parallel organisation, called the Road Racing Council (RRC) had been formed the year before the Wheelers. The RRC had first seen the light of day in 1922 but, by 1937 it would turn into the Road Time Trials Council (RTTC), becoming the de facto controller and record-keeper of time trialling throughout the UK. Initially it had been focused on the south of England and Midlands but, after complaints from the regions, the RRC was transformed into the nationally-minded RTTC. But, once again, we digress...

While the NCU and RTTC controlled British cycle sport through the 1920s – both time trial, track and closed-circuit mass start events – things were a little different north of the border. After initially following the regulations of the NCU and RTTC, Scottish clubs got together to form the Scottish Amateur Racing Association (SARA) in 1931. Given the rapidly changing and expanding world of cycling, by 1936 a meeting resolved to form a new body that would represent all racing called the Scottish Amateur Cycling Association (SACA), which promptly replaced SARA. There were already too many acronyms and not enough clarity about what organisations aims were, how big their memberships were or even, alas, a record of minutes and meetings.

For good measure, just as SACA was finding its feet in 1937, the NCU formed a Scottish section to try to regulate track events and mass start road racing, a competitive format for which there was increasing interest in the UK. The track and closed-circuit focused NCU had actually *forbidden* what we know now as road racing on open roads, so what few 'mass start' events the NCU did deign to sanction were always held on closed circuits.

Viewed at a distance – and even by many at the time – the effective banning of mass start road racing on open roads by the NCU was unfathomable. After all, such events had already been run on continental Europe for decades. A sport in which one of its most popular and heroic branches was effectively banned – by its own governing body rather than the police or government – is fatally handicapped even before the flag drops.

This bizarre NCU policy was in fact a hangover from an earlier era, that first cycling boom in the 1880s. Back then, the first UK governing body founded in 1878 was grandly titled the British Cycling Union (BCU). A precursor to the NCU, it had meekly rolled over faced with police and public pressure to stop cyclists *"riding furiously."* After a decade in which the cycling craze had taken off, the BCU – which was renamed the NCU in 1883 – attempted to keep cycling 'respectable' by adopting a resolution which stated, 'We desire to discourage road racing and call upon clubs to assist it by *refusing* to hold races upon the road.'

Given that draconian starting point it's not surprising that cycle sport – the one-day Classics and Grand Tours of continental Europe – struggled to gain acceptance on British roads. There's little chance of developing a deep-rooted cycling culture and sporting tradition if those in charge of racing try their best to prevent it from happening on British roads in the first place. What chance did any British road race have of ever weaving its way into the tapestry of national sporting events – a Yorkshire one day Classic – when the national body was against any such racing? Additionally, media coverage of mass start road races was paltry and often dismissive. It would take another book and analysis to fathom the long-lasting impact of that anti-road racing approach, an attitude that set the tone towards cycle racing in the UK for decades to come. Arguably, it lingers to this day in the approach of other road users who encounter cyclists on 'their' roads. So it was that throughout the early decades of the 20th Century the NCU focussed its efforts on track racing and early morning solo time trials, leaving 'mass start racing' out in the cold, labelling it a pariah sport and obviously stunting its growth.

Around the same time, to further cement the importance of solo time trialling, *Cycling Weekly* inaugurated the British Best All-Rounder (BBAR) competition in April 1930. As an aside it's also worth noting that the same magazine was staunchly opposed to road racing, refusing to cover any British 'massed start' race until 1944 at which point editorial opposition to the 'rebel' British League of Racing Cyclists softened.

The BBAR title was awarded to the rider who had recorded the best average speeds in time trials of 50, 100 miles and 12 Hours and it was considered a significant prize in British cycling sport for the next 60 years. It was only in the 1980s that the enthusiasm for long distance time trials began to fade from club life. Attempts to tweak the format to include the popular 25 mile distance failed to save the format's waning importance in British cycling clubs.

Given the economic importance of the bicycle industry in the UK and given the fact that it was a means of transport for millions of people in the 1930s, it's hard to understand why the NCU wasn't more militant when it came to asserting itself at the time. In the end, the NCU's backward, anti-road race attitude would prove to be its downfall.

Meanwhile, throughout those many seasons when the NCU attempted to stifle UK road racing, in mainland Europe, one-day Classics and the tours of Italy and France were inspiring Scottish riders to race. Of course a club *could* run a race, but those who took part risked long bans from the NCU. To be fair to the NCU, it did organise some road races, albeit on closed circuits and airfields – in 1933 at Brooklands in Surrey, while Donington Park and Mallory Park motor racing tracks also featured.

However, such was the strength of the prohibition against road racing that most riders stuck to racing in early morning time trials sanctioned by the RTTC. These crack-of-dawn races were all held amid bizarre levels of secrecy – the courses all had codes rather than names that did nothing to promote the sport. Thus, "W.A.2 – 25 miles. Start 35 revs south of Crash Gate entrance to aerodrome on Abbotsinch road," begins the description of one of Glasgow's 25 mile time trial courses. The scarcity of events and circuits as well as the hardships of the time – long working hours and no cars – meant riders generally raced locally.

Throughout the 1930s however, the clamour for 'mass start' racing increased still louder, given that it had become something of a 'fad' and news from continental Europe fanned road racing flames. Riders wanted to take part in road races – the problem being that the biggest British national governing body was still opposed to them.

One rider of the era, Londoner Ken Smith, recalled that in 1938 "I got hooked on the 'massed start' racing craze and rode in several events at Brooklands but without much success." The talk in 'Cycling' magazine was of the surge in popularity of 'the massed start game' and there was no stopping it. Legendary cycling journalist Jock Wadley wrote "Massed start....Here we are in 1937 in the midst of a revival of the earliest and most natural form of bicycle racing. The pioneers of the great game of cycling did not have much difficulty in deciding how they should match their athletic ability."

The London-based Wadley was an early advocate for road racing, writing for *The Bicyclist* magazine, which had been launched in 1936 in opposition to the long-running *Cycling* which was perceived as being anti-'mass start' and too close to the NCU establishment. For his part, as a fan of European Classics and Tours, Wadley noted that British riders were at a disadvantage when it came to world championships, since the British riders had almost uniquely ridden solo time trials and, when faced with riding in a bunch, they struggled with both bike handling and tactics.

It was in this atmosphere that the British League of Racing Cyclists (BLRC) emerged in 1942. If the NCU and its Scottish division weren't going to help develop road racing then the new BLRC was more than willing to take up cudgels for Scotland's frustrated roadmen. In spite of the rumblings of discontent for organising 'massed start' road races on British roads, none of the existing organisations had showed any enthusiasm to promote, in Wadley's words, the "most natural form of bicycle racing."

Looking back, its hard to grasp the depth of the rivalry – in fact the outright hostility – that existed between the competing factions, whereby new members of clubs were told that if they fraternised with the other side they would be in trouble. The idea that any competitive cycling organisation would actively campaign *against* road racing on open roads seems absurd, but of course that was literally what was happening throughout the 1930s. There seemed to be little common ground between the organisations.

There wasn't even broad unanimity between these various organisations – British or Scottish – and they certainly weren't all pulling in the same direction. It is a matter of record that when the first Duntocher-Dunoon road race was run in 1934 that SACA refused an application by the Cowal Games organisers. Needless to say the NCU refused too, stipulating it would only agree if fully-closed roads were guaranteed. Opposition be damned, the 1934 Duntocher-Dunoon went ahead on 30 July and was in fact the first-ever open road mass start event to be held on British roads, organised by Glasgow bike shop owner Adam Dale. The 'open road' description is important, because the week previously there had been another 'mass start' road race in Scotland, the 'Round Cumbrae cycle race' around the isle of Bute, but, since it was on a circuit on the island, it passed almost unnoticed by cycling historians.

Dales Cycles had been in business since 1912 and, like so many bike shops, supported local clubs, races and riders. The Duntocher-Dunoon event was part of the Cowal Highland Gathering, which every year tried to add a new novelty to its programme. The *Glasgow Herald* cycling correspondent sniffly wrote, "The second of the massed start events is over, and the crop of accidents in the Dunoon race far exceeds the number in the round Bute farce." Although the 'March of 1,000 pipers' was, apparently, the noisy highlight of the gathering. 50 riders took the start and the finish – on the grass of Dunoon Recreation Park – and saw Clarion rider Gilbert Hamilton win ahead of Glasgow Wheeler Tommy Potter (brother of Jackie) and A. O. Jones riding for Stockton Wheelers. This trio had broken clear on the Rest and Be Thankful climb and, although Potter was first into the park and led the sprint out, Hamilton came round him to claim a historic victory. Potter would remain a Wheeler for years, while Hamilton was killed while returning from a club run, hit by a car at Inchinan in the early 1960s.

Subsequently, BLRC founder Percy Stallard would claim that Britain's first-ever 'mass start' race on open roads was the Llangollen-

Wolverhampton which the Wolverhampton RCC organised eight years later, in 1942. Stallard's wholly inaccurate claim somehow went unchallenged and has now entered numerous cycling history books as established fact. Well, it might well have been the first 'mass start' race in England, but if we're talking about Britain and demanding historical accuracy, this is simply not true. Baldy stated, the 1934 Duntocher-Dunoon was the first open road race held in Britain. As with the development of the bicycle and the pneumatic tyre, Scotland was there at the start and the Glasgow Wheelers had a rider on that very first British road race podium!

National pride and petty point-scoring aside, the permissions fiasco around the 1934 Duntocher-Dunoon is a perfect illustration of the state of the cycle sport nation at the time. The report of the event in the broadsheet *Glasgow Herald* was sneering and disdainful in its tone. The Herald's regular cycling correspondent 'Ladep' was a committed fan of time trials and viewed 'the bunch game' with barely disguised horror. Having said that, Ladep did note that the trio "managed to climb the Rest and Be Thankful without dismounting" and Glasgow Wheeler Potter won the prime at the summit for his efforts. However, "Like the Bute event this race had its farcical side. The competitors were fed from motor cars, which on other occasions were used for pacing." Poor Ladep would have had a heart attack if he had watched modern stage racing.

Only four years later, in 1938, when the organisers of the Scottish Empire Exhibition proposed a three-day, 500 mile Tour of Scotland, finishing in Bellahouston Park on Glasgow's south side, SACA once again refused permission for the race to be run. For an organisation presumably interested in promoting bike racing and introducing it to the general public, it had a funny way of going about it.

Clearly road racing was a mess of competing and contradictory factions and would take the formation of Stallard's British League of Racing Cyclists in 1942 to precipitate real change (of which more in the next chapter). Even then there was more than rivalry between the NCU-affiliated clubs and those who opted for BLRC membership. There are credible stories of NCU members tipping off local police forces about races being run and plain clothes cops turning up on

Sundays to stop riders. This practice and enmity carried on up until the late 1940s.

Nevertheless, in spite of the obstacles, there was still road racing in Scotland and not all of it was unsanctioned! Among the Wheelers of the era, Jackie Bone was one of the star performers – and not just in Scottish terms. The son of a disabled serviceman who had first taken up cycling as a delivery boy in Milngavie, Bone joined the Glasgow United CC as a 19-year-old in 1934. Bone had 'got serious' and won his first '25' in his first year, at which point his cycling career took off.

On a baking hot day in 1935 Bone broke the British 12 Hour time trial record riding 244 and three-quarter miles on a course based on the 'coast' down towards Ayr and then back to Linwood for as many laps of a seven mile circuit as they could manage. "I rode well all day," Bone recalled in a later interview. "In fact I started so fast and kept it up over the first six hours that everyone said I was crazy. They thought I was sure to blow up long before the finish." At that point the 21-year-old Bone worked as a moulder in an iron foundry and we might speculate that the peculiarly warm day wouldn't have bothered him that much. It's said that back then the etiquette in a '12' was to actually stop and have something to eat, something Bone decided against, riding past the picnickers at Bishopton!

"The course had been checked to allow for a maximum distance of 230 miles," continued Bone, "Long before the end of the day it was obvious that I'd beat that, but the officials just nodded and kept saying 'He won't last.' I had less than an hour to go before they realised I wasn't going to crack and was certain to smash the British record. There was real panic then! When I had covered all that there was to do of the course they had planned I was directed back over the way I had gone in the morning. Then they sent me through Paisley town centre, up and down back streets, over cobbles. Three of four times I was turned into culs-de-sac and had to turn and come out again."

After nearly 12 hours of effort on record-breaking pace, its hard to imagine how Bone kept his calm and focus. "I was finally run out up a back street somewhere and told I had topped 244 miles. I am certain that if there had been a proper finishing circuit, like those used now,

I could have added another couple of miles to that at least." Of which there can be little doubt.

Bone's distance made him the first British rider to average over 20mph for a '12' and he did it on a 79-inch fixed wheel (roughly 52x17) and on several cobbled stretches. For the sake of accuracy we have to note that he also did it prior to joining the Wheelers and Bone was riding in Glasgow United kit that record-breaking day.

Bone was also the Scottish Best All-Rounder champion in 1935, riding a '50,' a '100' and a 12 Hour time trial with a combined average speed of 21.561mph. Time triallist of talent he may have been, but by the end of 1935 Bone had more or less finished with 'riding solo against the clock' and turned his attention to the increasingly popular 'mass start' racing. Jackie Bone had decided he was going to be a road racer. Better still, he was going to get selected for the inaugural Olympic Games road race to be held in Berlin in 1936.

"Well, I knew it was no good racing in Scotland and hoping that the selectors would hear about me," continued Bone, showing a precocious grasp of cycling selection politics, "so I decided to go south and fight for a place where they couldn't ignore me." Outspoken and not shy about his evident talent, Bone's results and aggressive riding style invariably saw him in the thick of the action. His campaign for selection saw him travel to the Isle of Man where he finished third in the inaugural lap around the island. The one-lap race – with a climb over the mountain made famous by the motorbike time trial (TT) races – was won by Charles Holland. Among the cognoscenti, the Isle of Man international was considered one of the toughest bike races in the UK. Not for Bone, who informed the organisers at the prize-giving that it was neither long enough nor hard enough. He said, "Take it three times around and it might start being tough." The following year the organisers would indeed add a lap and, in its heyday, 'the Manx' International would comprise three laps of the motorbike TT course.

Bone's efforts gained him selection for both the Olympics and the world championships in 1936. The Berlin road course was over the 'standard' 100km distance, but it didn't impress Bone. "There wasn't a hill worth the name in the entire race, as an Olympic test it wasn't hard enough for a women's area championship!" observed Bone whose race would end in a mess of malfunctioning gears and bloody road rash.

"The big bunch was still together four miles from the finish and I was near the head of it with Charlie Holland. It was obvious that we'd have to get right up to the front if we were to have a chance of winning. I saw a gap and went for it, but a Dutch rider beside me evidently had the same idea. We were racing for the gap when he suddenly leaned across and socked me on the jaw. I went down, wrecking my gears and tearing my tubular."

On the day, Bone kicked his gears back into shape and finished the race, fittingly ahead of the Dutchman who had, in turn, been punched by an Italian. The irony was that Bone himself was reported for 'ungentlemanly conduct' because he had refused a request to stop and help the injured Dutchman...

The 1936 Olympic road race was won by future Tour de France rider Robert Charpentier with French legend Guy Lapebie in second. Bone might have been a road racing rookie, but in that 1936 Olympic peloton, he was in exalted company. In truth, Bone was no stranger to disagreements with authority. In 1937 he was talked of as leader of the GB team at the world championships yet ended up being excluded after having 'words' with a selector.

In one of the four selection races that 1937 season Bone won at Alexandra Palace, incidentally laying claim to one of the more unusual 'firsts' set by a Glasgow Wheeler. Bone's win meant he won the first-ever road race *televised* in Britain.

On a course (conveniently) traced around the BBC television headquarters in Alexandra Palace in London, Bone won the 17-mile road race held in the hilly park, clipping off the front of a bunch that included Percy Stallard, Australia's Tour de France legend Hubert Opperman (the man who gave us the 'Oppy' cap) and Harry 'Shake' Earnshaw. Bone cleared off on the third of 11 laps and that was the last the bunch saw of him!

In the other three selection races that season Bone finished second on the Isle of Man, third in the national championship race around

Donington Park motor circuit and fourth at Brooklands car circuit in Surrey. Only Yorkshireman Jack Fancourt had better results yet, somehow, the Glasgow Wheeler was excluded from the GB world's team.

Illustrating that inter-club rivalries are as old as the sport, it has to be reported that Bone insisted he lost the 1937 Isle of Man race thanks to the efforts of his Glasgow Wheelers club mate Donald Morrison. Which is to say that on the final climb of the Mountain course, Bone had attacked and dropped Fancourt. At the summit, Bone had a 30-second lead which, for a time triallist of Bone's pedigree, should have been enough. Off the breakneck descent and run-in to the line, Bone looked back. "I couldn't believe it, when they came up with Donald at the front. I'd had it. I could never beat Jack Fancourt in a sprint, there was just four easy miles left to the finish and no chance of breaking away again."

Sure enough, on the long finish straight at Douglas, Fancourt led out the sprint, Bone was legless and Morrison five bike lengths further back. "I didn't even try to match Fancourt's big sprint," explained Bone, "I just wanted to beat Morrison. I was sore about what he had done on the mountain and was determined to beat him for it. It was a sad way for two clubmates to finish an international race." History does not record what Morrison's version of events was, but it looks like a chance lost for a Glasgow Wheeler to have won that famous race.

In any case the Wheelers won the 1937 Manx team prize with Bone, Morrison, Jimmy Brinkins and Willie Milne. The quartet were photographed, all sporting the classic Glasgow Wheeler jersey – white with a blue band around the chest and blue piping on neck and sleeves – bikes all featuring a single bottle, held in a cage on their bars, centre-pull brakes, spare tubs wrapped around their shoulders, all lean limbs and slicked down hair.

Next year, 1938, Bone was back in the international fold – having briefly contemplated a professional career and participation in the Tour de France – but the 1938 world road race championships were to be his last hurrah. When he returned from the Netherlands he discovered that he had lost his job. "The boss didn't like me being away so often racing," recalled Bone, "I could understand his point of view, but I was unemployed for three months and I had just got married." There was no social security or unemployment benefit in 1938, social security was still a decade off, so for a man like Bone, unemployment meant serious hardship. "I couldn't risk that happening again. Anyway, I was fed up racing. I hated training and the old sparkle had gone out of competition." Bone toured with his wife for a few years, but, at the age of 24, his racing career was over.

Happily for the Wheelers, the 'dastardly Donald' Morrison would pick up the baton left by Bone, while Jimmy Brinkins was coming on song too, with a young miner Alex Hendry starting to make a name for himself. Morrison went on to win the Glasgow-Dunoon in 1937, the last edition of the race to be run before the second world war stopped all serious play.

The world road championship – for amateurs only – had been run since 1921 by the Union Cycliste International (UCI) which had been attracting national federations since it was formed in 1900. The UCI had taken over from the International Cycling Association (ICA) – the latter had been in existence since 1892. The UCI had become the new global authority in cycling and the NCU, which had been a power broker in the earlier ICA, was forced to shift its allegiance to the UCI in 1903. Ironically, the UCI insisted that Great Britain could only enter one team – Great Britain – rather than one each from Scotland, England, Ireland and Wales. After dragging its feet for three years, the NCU caved in and signed up to the UCI. Which is why, to this day, Scotland doesn't 'exist' as a UCI-recognised international cycling nation. Internationally, Scotland emerges every four years, when it puts in an appearance at the Commonwealth Games before vanishing again from the international stage. It's like two-wheeled Brigadoon, where Scottish characters emerge from the rain and mist, but clad in dark blue lycra rather than garish Holywood plaid.

Among the racing Wheelers in the early 1930s, Morrison, like Bone, had been making a name for himself, performing well south of the border too, cranking out the sort of rides that got a man noticed by international selectors.

In the summer of 1937 the Morrison-Bone-Brinkins trio would break the Scottish 100 mile time trial team record (best three riders times added together) not once, but twice. Clearly in good form, Bone also set a new Scottish '30' record with a 1-16-40, a mark that stood for two years. For his part, Morrison also won the (Glasgow) Duntocher – Dunoon that summer. Whether riding in road races or time trials, this trio was a formidable band of performers, north and south of the border. In 1939, the same year Bone was selected for the world's, Brinkins set a new Scottish '25' mile time trial record at 1-01-54 – this in an era of grippy roads, little traffic to chase and no time trial bikes of course. The next Glasgow Wheeler to break the Scottish '25' record would be Graeme Obree, in his single-season flirtation with the club, in 1991. Obree's mark was 49-48, though it's fair to say that plenty had changed from when Brinkins posted his time, without considering the Obree's own idiosyncratic design innovations.

All of which performances help explain how Morrison was selected to race the World road championships in Italy in 1939. At that tumultuous point in cycle sport history it was still the NCU which selected riders to represent Britain. Since the Wheelers was affiliated to the national body, Morrison was in the frame. The news that a Scot had been included in the British team for the world championships was big enough to make the *Scottish Daily Record* sports page when it was announced in August of that year. Sadly, when the German army invaded Poland a few weeks later on 1 September, Morrison's ticket to Italy was cancelled. As, indeed, were the world cycling championships, which vanished into the fog of war, only organised again in 1946.

For his part, Morrison went off to complete his national service and was listed as a 'Service Member' of the club from 1940 through to 1942.

Needless to say the various privations of wartime saw the club membership shrink – there were only 16 senior members and two juniors on the books in November 1944. Curiously however, the second world war did have a positive impact on the development of road racing, in as much as those agitating for road races to be held on open roads realised that with petrol rationing and less traffic, now was the time to push. The man who was responsible for the foundation of the BLRC, Percy Stallard, a talented rider who had represented Great Britain internationally at the World road race championships in the 1930s – ironically selected by the NCU. Stallard, was, by all accounts a determined, argumentative 'awkward sod' and he wrote to the NCU in December 1941 insisting, "There would be no better time than now to introduce this form of racing to the roads, what with the decreased amount of motor traffic and the important part that the cycle is playing in wartime transport." Airfields, so long the location for NCU-sanctioned road races were currently occupied with Lancasters, Spitfires and the pressing business of anti-fascist warfare.

The NCU didn't care to get involved or change its position on road racing, so in due course Stallard set about organising a race from Llangollen to Wolverhampton on 7 June 1942, a 59-mile point-to-point race with 34 starters. Stallard sought and gained the police permission, which upset both the NCU and the Road Time Trials Council (RTTC), which had never asked the police for permission to race. The RRTC argument was that if you had to ask the police to race then what did you do when or if the police said 'No'?

Stallard's race went ahead and, according to *Cycling Weekly*, attracted a crowd of a thousand at the finish. Stallard and the other riders who took place were subsequently banned for life and, as war raged in Europe, cycle sport battle lines were being drawn up in Britain. Which side was the Glasgow Wheelers on?

Having been banned by the NCU for running a road race on the open road, Stallard and other agitators decided to cease negotiations and set up a rival organisation – the British League of Racing Cyclists (BLRC), widely knows as the 'League.' Initially, the BLRC actually consisted of three different regional Leagues – including London and the Midlands – but by the autumn of 1942, Stallard and his collection of like-minded riders met in the Buxton youth hostel to amalgamate and unleash the British League of Racing Cyclists. It seemed like a step forward to many, but the power struggle between the competing groups would endure for 17 long and squandered seasons.

The confusion, squabbling and downright enmity that existed between the organisation of road racing in the UK rumbled on throughout the 1940s, a waste of time and energy for all concerned. Clearly world war two forced cycling onto the back burner (and some bespoke frame builders closed due to shortages of steel which had been commandeered by the armaments and aerospace industry) but inter-organisational rivalry carried on regardless during the war years and, inevitably, Scottish clubs were involved.

In fact, there's no way to tell the history of the Glasgow Wheelers without reference to sport and cycling politics. As much as the majority of riders pedal, race and train in blissful ignorance of minutes, meetings and sock length regulations, the fact is that without organisations to run their sport, there wouldn't be an international sport to speak of – unless you'd be content with a club-confined 8.4 mile time trial or autumn hill climb out of Blanefield! For better or worse, various Glasgow Wheelers were deeply involved in the shenanigans that birthed modern Scottish – and British – cycle sport.

In Scotland, the impetus to affiliate with the 'rebel' BLRC was down in no small part to members of the Glasgow Wheelers, after all, their members had been racing on open roads for almost a decade before the BLRC had seen the light of day. In attendance at an early BLRC meeting held in Scotland in 1946 were Arthur Campbell, Alex Hendry, Pat McCabe, Chryston Wheeler George Edwards ("a 14 stone lampman at Cardowan colliery"), J. Pettigrew and J. Wallace. That's three Glasgow Wheelers who helped determine the future of road racing in Scotland and, by extension, Europe and the world.

Although the NCU was the national British organisation affiliated to the UCI at the time, the UCI was less than impressed by the way in which the NCU had 'supported' road racing, so much so that when the BLRC arrived on the scene, it was easy for the UCI to accept overtures from the 'rebel' road riders. The BLRC racing programme and outlook was far more in tune with that of the other member federations of the UCI, so the sport's direction of travel was clear to all – and it wasn't with the NCU.

Cannily, the BLRC had nailed its colours to the mast as soon as it had been formed in 1942. Its December statement that same year, "The policy of the BLRC is to encourage and promote in Great Britain all forms of amateur and professional cycling based on international practice and conformity with Union Cycliste Internationale (UCI) Rules. The League is willing to co-operate with other promoting bodies who are prepared to further this aim," could hardly have been more clear to whom and what style of racing it was focused on.

By 1946 – following the BLRC's organisation of its first Tours of Britain – the die was well and truly cast. The Wheelers had already signed up with the Scottish branch of the BLRC at a meeting on 3 March 1945 where Arthur Campbell, Alex Hendry and Pat McCabe were among the 15 bold souls present at an era-defining meeting. The Wheelers was 'a Leaguer' club. Other Scottish enthusiasts of 'the bunch game' didn't waste much time either. Credit must go too to George Edwards and the Chryston Wheelers – a 38 rider strong club at the time – which, like the Wheelers, also opted to affiliate to the BLRC in March 1945.

The clubs who formed that new section wasted no time in organising an event. Just three weeks later, on 25 March, it ran a race starting and finishing from Lennoxtown, taking in Kilsyth, Denny, Carron Bridge, Fintry, then over the Crow road and back to the finish. Alex Hendry, in a classic Glasgow Wheelers jersey, won the 32-mile race. After that road racing success, on 19 May 1945 – a month before the end of the second world war – the Scottish section of the BLRC ran another event on the same course with a prime on the Crow road. This time there were 32 entrants from the Glasgow, Gilbertfield and Chryston Wheelers, as well as riders from Blaydon RRC and the Northern Coureurs. The first prize was a 40 shilling value. That is to say a prize to the value of two pounds. A programme was printed and the 27 competitors included no few than *13* Glasgow Wheelers, including Hendry, George Edwards, Tommy Dick, Arthur Campbell, Stuart Montgomery and John Thayne.

A little over a year later, on Sunday 18 August 1946, the new road racing outfit put on the inaugural BLRC British national road race championship on Glasgow's south side. Among the listed officials were Judges Arthur Campbell, Joe Patterson, John Pettigrew and John Stewart, the recorder and 'machine examiners' were Willie Thayne and James McDougal and race announcer Andy McMahon. The race organiser was James Wallace (who was also the timekeeper) and, like all the others, he too was a Glasgow Wheeler. It's fair to say that the Glasgow Wheelers had a *big* hand in organising the first-ever BLRC national road race championship.

The 126 mile race started in Pollokshaws – the strip was in the old Pollokshaws baths on Ashtree road – and headed south west before looping back to finish in Thornliebank. It took in Stewarton, Fenwick, Kilmarnock, Mauchline, Auchinleck, Cumnock, New Cumnock, Kirkconnel, Sanquhar, the mighty Mennock Pass and Wanlockhead village. Clearly it was not a course for the faint-hearted, and was won by a new recruit to the Chryston Wheelers, George Edwards, in a time of five hours and thirty-nine minutes from 25 starters, among whom were a brace of Glasgow Wheelers – Jimmy Brinkins and Tommy Dick. There were only 25 starters because that was all that had been authorised. Nevertheless there was enthusiasm and interest, so much so that there were nine further reserves listed in the four-page programme (price thruppence, or one a half pence). Other than another Wheeler, James Brown, there were riders from Ealing, Teesside and Wolverhampton, regions where the BLRC was strong.

Even at this early stage in modern British cycle sport, Campbell had revealed himself as an organiser and, once that first band of Scottish riders and teams had decided to hitch their futures to the BLRC, it was Campbell whose name was prominent on BLRC Scottish literature. If there was a race start sheet, there would be an advert for the BLRC on it urging 'interested cyclists' to write to Campbell at 22 Garvald street in Dalmarnock.

It was clear to all – other than the NCU evidently – which way the wind was blowing. Fighting a doomed rearguard action, in 1946 the NCU in Scotland formed the Scottish National Cyclists' Union, affiliated, of course, to the NCU.

The die had already been cast and, at a meeting in the Clarion Rooms in Queen's crescent in Glasgow during December 1946, the

Scottish section of the BLRC changed its name and reconstituted itself, emerging as the Scottish Cyclists' Union (SCU). To really set the cat among the organisational pigeons, the new SCU decided to approach the UCI and ask for recognition as the governing body of cycling in Scotland. By 1953, having maintained contact and developed a network, Campbell was named as SCU delegate to the UCI international congress and made the trip to Lugano to represent Scotland – rather than England or Great Britain – at the UCI.

The first President of the new-born SCU was Tom Cook, by then a Labour MP for Dundee, but originally a miner from the Scottish cycling heartland of Larkhall in north Lanarkshire. Cook and Campbell exchanged correspondence and there's no doubt that Cook was a far-sighted pro-cycling advocate. Alas, in December 1945 he was up against Alfred Barnes a Labour Minister for roads and transport who was, in a manner of speaking, more NCU than BLRC. In a Ministry of War Transport letter to future SCU president Cook, Barnes wrote "...the Government is strongly opposed to the running of massed start cycle races on public highways, not only because of the dangerous conditions that they create, but because of the call they make on the time of the police... I hope that the BLRC will carefully reconsider this matter and will agree to stop running these races. If the Government's appeal proves to be insufficient I shall have to consider asking Parliament for the necessary powers to stop them." Sporting battle lines had been drawn in no uncertain terms and evidently the BLRC and SCU had no friends in high places, not even in the governing Labour party of Clement Attlee. Of course, less than a year later Stallard and the BLRC had organised the *third* 'Six-Day Cycling Marathon Brighton – Glasgow' with the assistance of Scottish riders, clubs and officials. Barnes might have disapproved, but he – and the NCU – were on the back foot. Barnes' threat of parliamentary legislation came to nothing, but his position had been backed by the Solicitor General and gives a flavour of the official antipathy surrounding cycle sport in those years. Not only was road racing opposed by the NCU, but the Labour government was threatening to ban it too. At this crucial point – even before the mass ownership of cars – cycling was fighting an uphill battle to find its place in British cultural and sporting life. It would never fully find acceptance.

A little more than 20 years after its formation, the Glasgow Wheelers had already featured prominently in the history of competitive Scottish cycling on road and track, domestically and internationally. Additionally, club members had been instrumental in shaping the organisation and politics of British road racing. Not a bad start for a cycling club. And, as it turned out, that was just the beginning.

3

CHANGING GEARS

THROUGHOUT THE 1930S, while rival federations, riders and event organisers had skirmished and plotted, life for the average Glasgow Wheeler went on as before. Not everyone was a Donald Morrison or a Jackie Bone, getting a Great Britain team call-up – the only call most riders would get would be to remind them that their club membership subs still hadn't been paid. And that 'call' would likely be in the shape of a letter, since by the end of the 1930s only around three million of the (roughly) 20 million homes in the whole of the UK had GPO-installed telephones.

Sadly, no annual general meeting minutes from the Wheelers remain from the 1930s, which means that names and many exploits have been lost. We should console ourselves by accepting that *every* history is only ever a partial one. However, thanks to John Thayne, who gathered information for an early web-based club history, we are able to remember several key figures.

Thus, we know that in the year of the club's formation – 1923 – that Pat (P.J.) McCabe joined the club and in a long competitive career, held Scottish track championship titles at all distances from one-quarter to three miles. Although Pat was not a founder, he was a member continuously until his death in 1993, with many years spent as club President or Chairman. In recognition of his efforts on and off the bike for the club, after his death the 'Pat McCabe Cup' confined championship was introduced and proved to be very popular. Other members who joined from the 1930s also included Jimmy Wallace,

James Thompson and Joe Patterson, the club's longest serving Secretary, though all were club stalwarts.

There's an argument – contested, inevitably, since it is backed by anecdote rather than hard numbers – that insists the years between the Wars were the heyday both of cycling in general and the Glasgow Wheelers in particular. There was plenty of racing and a contingent of strong riders from the Wheelers taking part. True, they were almost all time trials, but, according to then chairman John Stewart speaking in 1973, "in 30 open races in which the club took place in 1937, members had been fastest in 23 of them and 22 team prizes were won." During the later 1930s, its true that Jackie Bone, Donald Morrison, Willie Milne, Jack Potter, Jimmy Brinkins and Joe Gallacher were a collective force to be reckoned with on British, never mind Scottish roads.

One of the longest-serving clubmen from that era, Jackie Potter, who joined the club in 1927 as a 19-year-old, made a name for himself as a long-distance time trialist. In an era we imagine riders from Glasgow and district as being miners from Chryston or south Lanarkshire, Potter had been a hairdresser before he changed tack and went to work for 'Flying Scot' frame builder David Rattray in 1937. By that point Potter was already breaking records and, obviously, doing it on one of Rattray's finest frames. Rattray, incidentally, had been a member of the club since 1924.

Potter stayed with Rattray for 42 years, finally retiring at the age of 69 in 1979. Even then Potter was still riding and was a founding member of the Veteran Time Trial Association (VTTA) Scottish division in 1952. Potter died in January 2010, a few months shy of his own centenary.

However, back in 1935, young Potter had raised eyebrows by setting a Wheelers club record for the '100' in an early-season Edinburgh Road Club event. Riding a single speed bike he posted 4-47-24 on roads that, by today's standards, were 'heavy' to say the least. Potter's time was only 80 seconds off the Scottish national record and, at that point, was the third-fastest time in open Scottish competition.

A few seasons later, Alex Hendry – born in 1922 – was coming into his prime as a rider in a Wheelers jersey. Hendry was in fact from a cycling family and his brothers Jackie, Willie and Andy all raced too, albeit in St Christopher's CC colours. Hendry, a miner from Muirhead on the north eastern outskirts of Glasgow, was regularly swapping wins and placings in 25 and 10 mile time trials with his team mates Jimmy Brinkins, Morrison and Bone. Hendry was certainly one the best all-rounders the club ever had; in that he could win time trials, road races, hill climbs and track events and was the only member to hold all the club records in the same season. Nit-picking completists would correctly point out that Hendry didn't actually hold the '12' title, but since it hadn't been held that season, we can probably stretch the point.

Keeping track in the 1939 club racing records Hendry often noted 'Self' as winner or 'Scratch man' in the open events promoted by long gone clubs like the Westcott CC, the Gilbertfield Wheelers, the Cambuslang CC, the Caledonian and Richmond. If the clubs have vanished then the time trial courses were often – as today – traced around Inchinan and the Westferry on the flatter roads of Renfrewshire.

Hendry and his family would ultimately be forced to move to England when the pits around north Lanarkshire started to close down in the early 1960s. Which is why, in 1965, Hendry ended up racing for the Coventry CC.

Well, sort of. A rider called 'Alex Hardie' joined the Coventry club and raced in time trials and on the local Butts Stadium track. But Hardie was, in fact, Hendry. Hendry had actually taken out a professional race licence in 1952 and competed as an independent or 'pro' on track and grass track in an era when there were strict regulations designed to keep amateurs and professionals apart. The rules additionally prevented ex-pros reverting to amateur status and racing with amateurs again.

Unfortunately for former pro licence holder Hendry, he was recognised and banned from racing. Hendry was finally reinstated as an amateur on Saturday 13 April 1968 and lined up to race on Sunday 14 April in a Midlands 25 mile time trial. The veteran Hendry won a prize for second rider on handicap. Sadly, nine years later, Hendry died of a heart attack at the young age of just 55 in 1977, while still based in Coventry. The following season the Tour of the Campsies hilly time trial was renamed the Alex Hendry memorial, in recognition of a Wheeler who excelled in the hills and against the clock. A roadman's sporting time trial seemed like an appropriate memorial to the ex-miner who could – and did – do it all. A decade later the timed hill-climb up the Crow road was named after another Wheeler racing great, Jimmy Brinkins, who passed away in 1986.

Though, yet again, no written record is available, there's evidence of a Bilsland in the Glasgow Wheelers being part of a Scottish national team pursuit winning team in the 1930s. It was the first time a Bilsland would feature as a Scottish national champion though, of course, it wouldn't be the last. Alec, father of both Billy and Ian (as well as Alistair and Douglas), was the rider, though even Billy can't be sure of the year of his dad's championship, reckoning it was either 1938 or 1939.

Needless to say both the wider club scene and the Glasgow Wheelers had taken a hit during the War years between 1939 and 1945. Obviously, in Europe, the major races were suspended for the duration of the war, though there were still some domestic competitions in Scotland. Brinkins, now settled in Milton of Campsie, had set the Scottish national '25' record in 1939, just before the outbreak of the war in September, recording a 1-01-54.

With members carrying out national service and food rationing, things were tough wherever you looked and club membership dwindled in the mid-1940s to around 20 riders, including juniors.

If names and stories from the 1920s and 1930s are hazy, then happily the hardbound accounts ledger 'Membership book' with its first entry for the 1940-41 season, remains intact. Its spine is now strapped up and held together with brown packing tape, but it contains the names and addresses of some of Scotland's finest riders.

In total, 51 riders are listed that grim war-torn 1940-41 season, among them many who would go on to feature throughout the coming decades of Wheelers history.

There was still some low-key domestic racing during the war, though it was often confined to Army and Royal Air Force bases. Unsurprisingly, minds, energy and other resources were focused on more pressing matters. Unsurprisingly both the wider club scene and the Glasgow Wheelers had taken a hit during the War years between 1939 and 1945.

The Thayne clan, which would play such an important role in the club, is already listed in the shape of club secretary and treasurer Willie, as well as junior James Thayne. This is no surprise and during the tough years after the second world war the Wheelers – like so many other areas of civil and sporting society – struggled. It was during these years that the club was particularly indebted to Willie Thayne for holding the Club together in his capacity as Secretary, treasurer and competitor.

Money may have been tight and the roads poor in the 1930s and 1940s, but that didn't stop equipment being developed – and sought after – by Scottish riders. The 'between the wars' period saw a leap forward in new technology and equipment which may look primitive by today's standards, but at the time was considered cutting edge.

Thus, for all that the 'cracks' of the European professional peloton had been using derailleur gears since the late 1930s, there was no settled design and the first winner of the Tour de France to use a rear mech had only been in 1937, when Roger Lapebie used a 'Globo Super Champion' design to win overall by seven minutes. Although various primitive two or three speed gear changing systems had existed for several years, the Tour organisers banned the use of a derailleur until 1937 which rather hindered their spread outside the European peloton, as well as their technical development.

World war two had inevitably put a brake on all sorts of bike and component developments. Domestically, frame building had all but came to a halt during the war years. Production at Reynolds steel earmarked for lightweight race bikes was – unsurprisingly – switched to turning out tubing for the air plane industry. Thus Rattray's production of its Flying Scot went into hibernation in 1941.

Post-War, businesses slowly started to get back into the groove, and the rear mech started to be more widely seen, even in Scotland. By the end of the 1940s, bike design and gear-shifting technology looked very much like it would for the next forty-five years.

But French-made rear mechs weren't the only objects of desire making their way into shops in the late 1940s. Although the world war in Europe had come to an end in June 1945, food rationing was still in force in Scotland until 1954 and there weren't many bananas to be seen sticking out of cycling jerseys during those years. There had been some respite in 1949 however, as sweets and chocolate were no longer rationed, even if demand outstripped supply. In truth, a combination of black market and home-grown vegetables meant that – if you had the money and the connections – there were ways to supplement what your ration book entitled you to, but for a serious cyclist with peculiar nutritional needs, the immediate post-War years were a challenge.

By the late 1940s there had been an upswing in the interest in cycling as life slowly returned to normal, though cycling was far from being exclusively competitive focused, an attitude encouraged by the recent formation of a new 'chain' of overnight accommodation. The Scottish Youth Hostel Association (SHYA) which had been formed in 1931, took off in popularity and cycling clubs were an integral and enthusiastic part of that growth. After all, given its remit – "To help all, but especially young people of limited means living and working in industrial and other areas, to know use and appreciate the Scottish countryside" – it was perfect for the average cyclist of the period. Barely five years after the formation of the SYHA there were 48 hostels in Scotland and a membership of nearly 12,000 adventurers hiking and riding around the country.

Although those cyclists of a touring bent already enjoyed support from the Cyclists' Touring Club (CTC) which had been founded during the first cycling boom in 1878, most Glasgow club riders opted to mix their riding, happily touring on weekends where there were no races to take part in. Scottish clubs, including the Wheelers, would readily promote road races and mid-week time trials, seeing the same members strap on a saddle bag and head for the Borders or to the north West for a weekend of hostelling.

But whether riders were more interested in racing or simply getting out to the countryside, the 1940s saw the Glasgow Wheelers grow as a club. The members who had been called up during the war or who were carrying out obligatory National Service in the armed forced were included as 'Service members' when they were away, paying their membership fees. 18 months of National Service was compulsory in the UK until 1963, having been introduced in 1948 and, though it meant living away from home, a number of riders from the era would still compete at inter-services sporting events, with road races being held on flat courses traced around barracks, airfields and parade grounds. It was hardly Paris-Roubaix, but it was better than nothing. War and shortages there may have been, but there were still 51 registered Glasgow Wheelers at the start of the 1940s in what was to prove a tumultuous decade in all sorts of ways, both sporting, local and, obviously, global. Affiliation to the newly-formed British League of Racing Cyclists (BLRC) organisation cost the Wheelers five shillings in 1945, George Edwards, the Chryston miner, was (briefly) on the membership roll, as was Arthur Campbell, who had made his first appearance in the Glasgow Wheelers records as a 25-year-old in 1943. Lest it be thought that Campbell was joining the biggest club or most powerful club in Scotland (far less Glasgow), in the middle of war, the Wheelers membership comprised only 22 other members. Senior members paid nine shillings (45 pence) but this was often paid up in instalments, all recorded in the membership book. As a sign of his commitment to his new club Campbell splashed out another one shilling and ninepence for his club 'cloth badge' in addition to his membership subs.

By way of comparison, in 1945 the Chryston Wheelers annual subscriptions were only five shillings (25p), junior club members – under 14 – paid three shillings (15p), while under 14s could ride with the club, so long as they were accompanied by a guardian. Clearly riding for the Glasgow Wheelers came at a premium!

In either case, neither fee sounds like a lot of money, even at a time when weekly average pay in that era was still only £7. Labour records show that a Falkirk clay miner, working five and three-quarter days a week was offered seven pounds and 13 shillings (£7.65) in November 1951. By then, one of David Rattray's lightweight steel lugged Flying Scots cost between £10 and £20 depending on wheels, chrome and components, where a roadster-commuter could be had for £5. And if you couldn't afford that, there was always the local bike shop's generous credit terms and you could get your dream bike on tick, on the never-never over a two year term. To be fair, one hundred years ago innovations, though plentiful, rarely attained universal acceptance, standardisation was some years off and mass manufacturing of quality racing components was in its early stages.

While the second world war had inflicted all manner of losses and privations, cycling had ticked over, domestically so, even before the war in Europe finally ended in May 1945, riders were keen to re-start club and racing life. After six years of conflict and shortage, there was a lot of pent-up enthusiasm for the sport.

In 1945 the desire to race would drive riders to what, today, would seem like extreme measures. In 1945 it was almost obligatory to ride to race starts, a practice that remained commonplace for many decades. However, riding to a race start in the Midlands from Glasgow did seem to be pushing it, even in 1945.

However, that is precisely what four Glasgow Wheelers did in order to ride the Circuit of the Clees, a 98 mile road race, organised by the Wolverhampton Racing Cycling Club. Arthur Campbell, Alex Hendry, George Edwards and Stewart Montgomery all rode down to race. Apparently the day before the race they visited Percy Stallard's bike shop and were more or less laughed out of it, having been told they had no chance. Edwards demurred, muttering that 'one of us is going to be first across that line tomorrow.' Sure enough, in front of a crowd of 4,000 Edwards outsprinted Hendry by a wheel after the two Wheelers had left the cream of British road racing two minutes behind in their wake. Stallard's post-race comments are not recorded. Perhaps, for once, the garrulous Stallard was lost for words, having only finished ninth, three and half minutes behind the Wheelers duo. Arthur Campbell 'got round' too, finishing 28th.

Capitalising on that optimistic mood, the British League of Racing Cyclists – formed at the end of 1942 – wasted no time. By summer 1945, after organising two smaller regional stage races in previous years, the BLRC went all-in and decided to organise what they thought would be a morale-boosting Tour of Britain between 6-10 August. A sporting tonic for a war-weary and battered nation.

After the European armistice was signed on 8 May 1945, the enterprising and patriotically-minded BLRC decided to run the 'Victory Cycling Marathon' between Brighton and Glasgow just three months later. By all accounts the race was a chaotic affair, stage distances were 'approximate' and riders had to find their own accommodation in each stage finish town. Legendary cycling journalist Chas Messenger wrote that, "No one had ever put on a stage race in this country…and even fewer people had ever seen one. Nobody knew what they were doing. The officials were inexperienced and their resources were being taxed to the limit." Chaos or not, the BLRC was savvy enough to present a letter to King George IV at Buckingham Palace prior to the start of the second stage. It was a smart bit of public relations and the stunt garnered publicity for both the race and the BLRC.

Given establishment opposition to racing on open roads, it was quite a coup for Percy Stallard's BLRC which noted that "the object of the League, namely, the development of healthy competition and friendly rivalry in cycling events may proceed unhampered." Two days later the race organiser James Kain received a letter from the Palace saying, "The King will be grateful if you will convey to the members of the League his sincere thanks for this Address, the terms of which he much appreciates." Take that NCU! Among the four-rider delegation at the Palace that day in 1945 – the rider who handed the 'Loyal address' letter – was Glasgow Wheeler Alex Hendry, the miner from Muirhead.

Hendry was one of four Scots and three Wheelers taking part in that first 'Marathon.' The others were Arthur Campbell and Stewart Montgomery, while George Edwards of the Chryston Wheelers was doing more than making up the numbers.

That inaugural five-stage, five-day event had started in Brighton with 99 riders and finished in Glasgow (in Carntyne), taking in Putney, then north out of London to the BLRC strongholds of Wolverhampton, Bradford, Newcastle and Glasgow.

The race was dominated by overall winner Robert Batot's French team and he won in 25 hours 22 minutes and 57 seconds, almost six minutes clear of runner-up Geoff Clarke of Bradford. Edwards was fourth on the final stage into Glasgow in front of a crowd said to number five thousand.

However, from a Wheelers perspective the star of the race was Alex Hendry, winner of stage four, a hilly 104 mile trek between Wolverhampton and Bradford. Unfortunately for Hendry his rear wheel collapsed two days later on the final stage to Glasgow on the summit of Carter Bar. Since there was no race service to help riders with mechanical issues, he had no option but to abandon. Montgomery got to Glasgow in 25th, while Campbell – wearing 'lucky' number 13 – had had to abandon in horrific weather conditions on the second stage.

Prize monies from that first Tour went unpaid for months and the event almost bankrupted the BLRC, but the event was run, the riders made it from Brighton to Carntyne and helped put British cycling on the European sporting map. Nevertheless, in 1945, the UCI still recognised the NCU as Britain's national cycling federation and, despite running the Tour of Britain, the BLRC was still the outsider and would remain so for another decade.

The following seasons saw Hendry and Edwards return and repeat their successes in the BLRC's national Tour, completing a one-two in 1946 on stage four (again into Newcastle, clearly Hendry's happy hunting ground) while Edwards won the final stage of between Edinburgh and Glasgow. It should also be noted that Glenmarnock CC lynchpin John Storrie was third on stage five! On the final overall classification, Hendry stood on the second step of the podium with Edwards in 12th.

In the official programme of the race – costing 6d (or two-and-a-half pence) – both Hendry and Edwards were big enough hitters to merit a mini-biography. Edwards was listed as George Edwards, Chryston Wheelers. Colours; Royal Blue. Age 23. Started cycle racing 1940. Weight, 13-st. 3-lb. Height, 6ft. Scottish road race and time trial champion, 1945. Winner, Trossacks (sic) road race, 1945. Winner, Star road race 1945. Winner, Clees road race, 1945. Winner, Glasgow-Edinburgh and back road race, 1945. Seventh five-day race 1945. Winner, Scottish Novice track championship, 1940. Fastest '25' miles 1h 2m 25s. Fastest "50" miles 2h 8m 47s, 1945. Considers his best performance finishing Five-day road race, 1945. Seventh in 25h 41m 23s (First Scotsman to reach Glasgow). Scottish road race champion, 1946.

For his part, his team mate was: Alex Hendry Glasgow Wheelers C.C. Colours, White with four-inch blue band. Age 25. Started cycle racing 1938. Weight, 10st 10lb. Height, 5ft 7in. First, Campsie road race. First, Deaut road race. First, Dechmont road race. First, Chryston Grand Prix road race. First, Glasgow to Dundee Victory road race. First, Carluke road race. Considers best performance Second in Circuit of the Clees by half-wheel to G. Edwards. First, Scottish section T.T. champion, 1946. 1945, Hill climb champion.

Also down on the start list in that 1946 program was Arthur Campbell, though he offered no *'palmares'* for our consideration, merely that he was number 19, while another Wheeler, Stewart Montgomery, was back for more too, as was the effervescent Storrie.

In 1947 the Wheelers contingent was back and Hendry won again, this time into Edinburgh after a tough ride up from Newcastle. It's a testimony to the enthusiasm of the riders as well as their qualities that they were welcomed back by the organisers. Scottish riders in a national tour who weren't just there to provide some local colour and bulk out the field. Both Edwards and Campbell would participate – as part of a a Glasgow Wheelers quartet which included Hendry and Montgomery – in a race that would eventually become the Tour of Britain. It was an event that would have a transformational effect on British cycle racing and its organisation, though nobody knew that at the time. Chaotic or not – unpaid prize money or not – that first national Tour, 'organised' by the BLRC created enough of a buzz in Scottish cycling circles for 12 clubs to abandon the NCU and hitch their wagons to the nascent BLRC. As an event, the 'Marathon' may have left much to be desired, but it signalled the future of British cycle sport and Scottish clubs and riders were intent on being in on it. The publicity boost given the stage racing by the event – as well as the epic nature of the undertaking had caught the interest of many and not just cyclists. The future of competitive cycling in Scotland would include road racing, no matter what the NCU board members wanted.

The popularity of that event and the boost it gave road racing shouldn't have come as a surprise, because road racing in Scotland was already part of the cycling scene. Consider, for example, that the Rothesay September weekend cycling festivals actually got underway with a road race held on the isle of Cumbrae in 1943 – two laps of the island course won by Alex Hendry who covered the 42 miles in 2-48-10. It was an event that had a long history, with the first version of the race held *before* the famous first Duntocher – Dunoon in 1934. However, given it was two laps of a closed road circuit on an island, it doesn't quite qualify as the 'first' road race on open roads.

However, by the end of the world war two there were even junior races being held on public roads. The first ever Scottish national junior road race was held in 1945, with the finish line chalked in the road. A few enthusiastic supporters witnessed a tight two-up sprint for that first title. It was a sprint between two Glasgow Wheelers, Alex Calder and Robert Thayne, won by Calder. A promising beginning for those young Wheelers.

Five years after the war ended, life slowly returned to something approaching normalcy and club membership had swelled to 115 of which seven were women. By the 1950s, senior club members were paying 10 shillings or juniors five shilling club subs, while in 1950 a Scottish National Cycle Union 'insurance and racing licence' was seven shillings on top of that. The annual turnover of the club's finances was somewhere between £30 and £40 and the club books of the period record spending on 'Cloth' or 'metal' or buttonhole badges, trophy engraving and, the biggest expense of all, the rental of the club room. In 1952 the club was meeting at a Rangers Supporters club room, paying the princely fee of £5.00 per annum, dallying a while in the Thornliebank Flute Band hall in 1954 before settling in the YMCA in 1955.

With the formation of the BLRC late in 1942 and the swift organisation of a Scottish branch shortly after, those Scottish clubs that had rallied around the BLRC banner would turn into a reconstituted Scottish Cyclist's Union (SCU) in 1952. However, given the fuzzy history, all that can said with certainty was that there are SCU handbooks going back to 1949 (at least) and that in that

1949 handbook, the Glasgow Wheelers are in there, the contacts are Joe Patterson and John Thayne and the club colours, somewhat surprisingly, are listed as blue, white and red.

In 1952 there was what might be called 'a general regrouping' when the various organisations amalgamated and by which point the club's colours had settled on 'White, blue band.' Thus, the Scottish clubs affiliated to the BLRC, the Scottish Amateur Cycling Association (SACA) and the Scottish National Cyclists Union all joined to form the Scottish Cyclists' Union – the SCU – which would run road, track and time trialling in Scotland. On 8 December 1952 the meeting to formalise the new organisation took place in the rooms of the Glasgow Clarion cycling club, in Queen's crescent in the west end of Glasgow. The first chairman of the new united Scottish body was none other than Arthur Campbell. Having been an active rider, Campbell had made plenty of connections and he had nailed his colours to the BLRC early on. When the BLRC boat came in, Campbell was well positioned to take the helm.

In the wake of the newly reformed SCU, in 1953, things were looking rosy for the Wheelers. Listed in the membership book that year were were no fewer than 121 members – the peak membership figure for the club – and subs had gone up to 15 shillings. The Thayne family was well represented that year (John, Bobbie and Alex, William and 'Baldy' – although Baldy Thayne's address was simply listed as 'America' which must have made contacting him tricky...), 'Jim' Dorward was on the books too, though Ian 'Steely' Steel had moved into the Independent pro realm. Recently elected SCU President Campbell and Jimmy Brinkins were still paying their 15 shilling subs too.

The formation of the SCU was a welcome development, offering much-needed stability. Throughout the 1950s the 'war' between the NCU and BLRC had reached new heights of absurdity. If the bickering seemed ridiculous, it had some serious consequences. Thus, when the Daily Express sponsorship for the nascent Tour of Britain was lost in 1952 it was as a direct result of intra-organisational squabbles and arguments. The head of publicity at the Express, Albert Asher, was so disgusted by the behaviour of the organisations that he pulled his newspaper's support and switched to the Formula 1 racing which was also getting back underway after the privations of the war years. Another example of cars coming out on top over bikes. It was ever thus! In any case, it was increasingly clear that the NCU was fighting a rearguard action to maintain its pre-eminence. There were even stories of NCU members 'tipping off' local police to inform them that there would be an illegal road race taking place on a certain time and date. With the Road Time Trials Council controlling the sport of time trialling and the NCU starting to come round to the idea of limited massed start road racing, the sport was still in a state of flux. With the BLRC gathering strength and membership numbers, the international body – the UCI – was becoming more and more kindly disposed to the 'rebels' of the BLRC and, by default, taking the SCU seriously. The problem was that the League was less well organised than either the NCU or RTTC and, administratively, it was a car crash. Peace talks were in the air. Curiously, although the BLRC was the more militant and vociferous organisation, it was a relative minnow, a two-wheeled guerilla insurgency taking on the Establishment. In 1943 the total *British* membership of the road racing enthusiasts of the BLRC only numbered around 450 souls. Change was in the air, in all sorts of areas. In the post-war 1940s, as the country had crawled out of the ruins of an economy with its material shortages, the decimation of the fighting-age population and ongoing food rationing – in short, the legacies of war – it took years to readjust. Recall that more than half of Great Britain's gross domestic product had been focused on war production and you get an idea of the impact on the population and sport. However, after years of war shortages productive energies were now turned towards peacetime objectives and Britain's trajectory was now, finally, upward.

With the introduction of the modern welfare state – free health and dental care, an end to means-tested unemployment benefit – by Clement Attlee's Labour government in 1948, life was improving for everyone. So much so that a barely decade later, Conservative prime minister Harold McMillan put down a heckler with his famous "You've never had it so good!" riposte.

Which short paragraphs offer an explanation for the increased affluence and security which, in turn, led to more cycling. As the 1950s got into their stride, the Glasgow Wheelers were on the up and up too.

4

CRAWLING FROM THE WRECKAGE

AS LIVING STANDARDS and wages rose in the 1950s, the quality of lives in Glasgow and beyond improved. Rationing ended in 1954, unemployment levels were at historic lows, the twin-tub washing machine, the television and fridge freezer became more commonplace in homes. And the 1950s saw the introduction of both the teabag and the transistor, which paved the way for cheaper 'radiograms' on which 'teenagers' could enjoy 'rock'n'roll' music while enjoying a leaf-free cuppa.

In all seriousness, socially, culturally and economically, Britain was changing. True, there was still a hangover from the shortages of the war and the early 1950s were far from glorious, but the mood was optimistic, the road ahead was clear.

You might expect that, with newfangled time-saving domestic appliances becoming more affordable, that there would be more women riding and racing? Culturally, the 1950s saw a big shift in attitudes to women and work, in fact, the 'role' of women. Given that women had demonstrated their abilities in all manner of traditional men's roles during the war, it was clear they weren't all going to abandon their independence and new-found economic clout to go meekly back into their old roles as 'wife and mother.' The gender once considered fit to be 'home makers' had helped win a world war and the self-confidence gained would not be dissipated.

So where, in this history, through all these years, are Glasgow's women riders? When you study those black and white photographs of club championship presentations, literally decades of riding and racing, you realise that there are no women in the frame. At best, one or two can be glimpsed in the dark backgrounds around tables at club dinners but, if there were women racing in Scotland in the early decades – or even in the 1950s and 1960s – they weren't doing it in Glasgow Wheelers colours. And make no mistake, women *were* racing.

This isn't simply because, 'Well, women didn't race back then,' given that in 1954 Eileen Sheridan was fast enough and famous enough to feature on the front cover of the SCU handbook in a Dunlop advert. Perhaps they were all riding for the Clutha Ladies CC?

In fact there were no fewer than 37 clubs in the West of Scotland Centre (the Rutherglen Nomads, the Gilbertfield Wheelers, Glasgow Transport CC, the Stamperland Wheelers...) in 1954 so there were plenty of clubs to chose from. By 1957 Beryl Burton had well and truly arrived as an international force too. Were there *no* racing women at all in the Glasgow Wheelers in the first 35 years?

In the Wheelers membership book, there are a few names peppered in the 1950s, and almost all are 'attached' to menfolk. Those 'solo' names that do appear – May Freeland, Irene Blacklock, June Cuthbertson, Janet Glasgow, Isabel Reid – rarely stayed in the club for more than a season. Of their racing activities, there is no trace though, to be fair, the same could be said of most of the male riders in the club. After all, not every member of the Wheelers was a race winner.

Others – both women and men – left their mark on the club by dint of their loyalty and longevity though and, when there were a few results thrown into the mix, well, so much the better.

Johan – pronounced Joan – Thayne, was the wife of John, mother of Iain, and so, in many ways, attached to the Glasgow Wheelers. Johan was, in fact, one of the first women members of the club. Speaking in her eighty-sixth year, Johan reflects simply that "women weren't asked to join, you just weren't encouraged to join the club. There really weren't many women – Avril Rankin, whose husband was in the club, and George and Gail McLean – but there weren't many women. At the time the Johnstone Wheelers had more women members and more women racing. Rita Jones (later Montgomery) was there of course and I think that attracted other women to join the Johnstone, because they had active (women) racing members. So you had riders like Grace Brierley and Myra Robertson in the Johnstone." In short, there were so few women in the Wheelers because they weren't made that welcome and if you were an ambitious racing woman, of course you would join a club where there were already women racing. Johan's name first appears as a member in 1961. Her husband, John had been a member since 1946, a Wheeler to his toe straps.

"I remember going down to the Rothesay weekend, before I was married, and Jimmy Dorward said to me 'I hope you're not here to distract my boys.' Imagine that. Those were his exact words, I'll never forget them. In the winter the Wheelers and the Glenmarnock would hold dances in Glasgow and everyone would go along, but you weren't really encouraged to do much, beyond being social in the winter." In cycling circles, women were often seen as mere decoration and distraction.

In the end, attitudes towards women in sport – and women in the Glasgow Wheelers – changed. It wasn't as if Johan was going to be holding anyone back or getting in the way. At 86 she still has her road bike set up on the turbo trainer at home, even if the 2023 roads are too intimidating. "We used to get home from work and the bikes would be all ready, we'd jump on and pedal up to Perth Youth hostel to all meet up. Whoever got there first put the kettles on. Then, next day, we'd all ride up to Inverness, the day after it was across to Fort William and then back down the road again on Monday – that was an Easter weekend with the Wheelers."

Inevitably – inevitable given all those miles that Johan and John were racking up – Johan turned out to be a formidable time trialist in the 1970s and 1980s though, she confesses rather sheepishly, "I only ever raced one '100' though. Although I caught John (Thayne) that day," she chuckles.

Perhaps the absence of women at the club, their struggle for acceptance and recognition can be seen as a reflection of the wider tumult of the post-war decades. Throughout the 1950s, the BLRC and NCU bickering buzzed endlessly, but the road racing genie was out of the bottle and there was nothing the NCU could do to convince anyone that – really, honestly – they were all for it.

In the background – and not unconnected to these federation shenanigans – a Glasgow rider named Ian Steel quit the Glasgow United to join the Glasgow Wheelers in 1950. We can't be coy about this, since Steel's move was motivated partly because the Wheelers had affiliated to the BLRC and this 'rebel' organisation had better relationships with stage and road race organisers in Europe than the NCU. Thus, teams and riders from BLRC-affiliated clubs tended to get international racing experience, sending teams to continental events like the Peace Race (Warsaw-Berlin-Prague), which Steel would famously win in 1952.

Steel's cycling career started in the mid-1940s and he quickly showed talent racing against the clock. Ian Steel, of '38 Hardridge road, Glasgow' pops up in the membership ledger of 1950-51, as having paid his 10 shilling subscription as well as his 2/6 – two shillings and sixpence – 'joining' fee. Steel joined the same year as James 'Jimmy' Dorward, but by 1952-53, Steel's name had gone from the ledger, though by then he had won both the Tour of Britain and the Peace Race, so its safe to say he was well-known beyond Glasgow club cycling circles!

Steel's brief dalliance with the Wheelers – lured by the club's connection to the BLRC and his close friendship with John Brierley – paid off. Rather than the NCU, it was the BLRC which was in contact with the organisers of the Peace Race, the famously tough tour raced between Berlin, Warsaw and Prague. The NCU's long antipathy to the 'bunch game' had meant it was the ramshackle but enthusiastic BLRC which had organised that first Tour of Britain back in 1945. That bold initiative had made international organisers take note of the fledgeling British outfit, so much so that other federations began to contact the BLRC looking for teams and riders to invite to races on continental Europe.

Thus, since the Wheelers was affiliated to the BLRC rather than the NCU, Steel signed up to ride, reasoning, in part, that it would open other doors. Sure enough, in 1952 the man who had formed the breakaway BLRC, Midlands firebrand Percy Stallard, took a six-man team to the Peace Race which included Steel (still a member of the Glasgow Wheelers at that point) and he became the first, last and only British rider to win one of the toughest most prestigious stage races in the sport. The NCU had been invited to send a team but, being far removed from the realities of road racing, had diplomatically and quite sensibly declined to send a team of time trialists, leaving Stallard's BLRC to snap up the invite.

Steel's switch to a BLRC-affiliated club was not just driven by a simple desire to race abroad, because Steel and fellow road racers understood what was required to road race, in the widest sense. On his return from Prague, Steel wrote, "Riding in BLRC road races has taught us a lot about team tactics and individual work in multi-stage racing, and the experience we have all gained from these events, especially in last year's Tour of Britain, was a telling factor in our ultimate success."

Steel and the British team won around £2,000 worth of goods, "including brief cases, watches, cameras, radio sets, shaving and toilet goods. And, to cap the lot, I won a bicycle which I gave away to a Scotsman living in Prague," recalled Steel.

The NCU decision to offload the Peace Race invite to the BLRC turned out to be the latest in a long line of missteps by the organisation, since Steel's victory with a BLRC team made the UCI prick up its ears. Consequently the UCI began taking the BLRC more seriously – or at least *as* seriously – as the NCU which had hitherto been seen as the de facto British cycling federation. Between the squabbling among the RTTC, BLRC and NCU, the UCI was getting the hump and muttered that 'Team' GB would be better off getting its act together. It would take another seven years of meetings before that eventually happened.

In 1953 the NCU finally dropped its ban of BLRC riders – including racing members of the Glasgow Wheelers – but it still forbade 'mixed' racing, meaning that BLRC affiliated riders couldn't take part in NCU events until 1957.

In Scotland, when the SCU was formed in 1952, it had immediately thrown in its lot with the BLRC, in part down to the enthusiastic lobbying and networking of Arthur Campbell. Clearly something had to change and with the Union Cycliste International (UCI) also now recognised by the International Olympic Committee (IOC), the jig was up. When the UCI and IOC were in accord, any federation interested in taking part in cycling on a global stage had better fall in line – there was no future for international cycling outside the powerful IOC/UCI sphere of influence.

With the increasingly well-organised IOC involved, forces more powerful than the SCU or BLRC were now in play and a longer, more pragmatic approach was required if the UK wasn't to become isolated from European road cycling.

Heads were cracked and talks held and, in February 1959, the NCU and BLRC agreed to amalgamate to form the British Cycling Federation – the BCF. Some protagonists, including BLRC founder Stallard, felt that the BLRC had sold out, but few club riders were overly concerned – when were racing cyclists ever interested in rules and bureaucracy? This new BCF would run road and track cycling in the UK until the arrival of rich Lottery funding in 1997 saw the organisation transformed into British Cycling (BC).

In any case, almost inevitably, there was a Glasgow Wheeler in the room when the BCF first saw the light of day. And, of course, it was Arthur Campbell, the committee man and cycling politician par excellence, who was there to represent the SCU. George Miller, himself a future president of the Scottish Cyclists' Union, was on the train going down to London for a BCF meeting in 1966, just seven years into the formation of the organisation. Miller was only 28-years-old. "I was there with Arthur Campbell and (fellow Scot) Gerry McDaid and on the way down we had discussed the minutes and what we wanted to say. It was my first BCF meeting and, as we got near London, Arthur slipped a piece of paper to me and said 'I want you to stand up, introduce yourself and ask this question. Then just sit down and it'll all go from there.' I was a bit confused, I didn't know what he was up to, but I did what he asked and, later, I realised that what he was doing was getting me noticed, 'introducing' me to the rest of the delegates. It was part of my training, as far as he was concerned. (Arthur) Campbell was a very skilful politician, I think he would have done a fantastic job in Westminster, I really do," recalls Miller.

If there were changes afoot in committee rooms and federations, there was movement too in the more practical side of riding and racing. For reasons of cost, many club riders were still on single-speed and single-speed fixed gear road bikes, though various geared options were becoming more widely available. A rear wheel with just three sprockets (a 16-19-22 block for example), a rear derailleur with a single 46 tooth front chain ring was not uncommon either. By the mid-1950s, many riders were on five-speed derailleur gears front and rear, though Simplex was the dominant brand of the late 1940s and early 1950s. However, the Campagnolo Gran Sport made its first appearance in Italy in 1951, and, by 1953, there was an entire Campag Gran Sport *'gruppo'* as the Italian firm established its products as objects of desire for the next 30 years.

On the Scottish domestic front around the same time, the boundlessly enthusiastic John Brierley was enjoying his best seasons and inspiring those around him. One of his *protégés* Alfie Fairweather, turned out to have a particularly long and successful career in the Wheelers which he joined in 1957. Originally from Cranhill, Fairweather recalls that his first bike a second-hand "wreck of a Raleigh for £2.00" although that didn't stop him riding it to Arbroath at the age of 13 – albeit he was accompanied by a cycling pal who was all of 18-years-old. A few years later, when the 17-year-old Fairweather started work at Barclay Curle shipyard, he met Brierley and was delighted to discover that Brierley knew Ian Steel and had been the best man at the Tour of Britain winner's wedding. The young Alfie had gone to see the stage finish of the 1951 Tour of Britain in Glasgow and saw Steel, and although rather star-struck recalls taking photos of Steel warming up at Glasgow Green before the stage start to Newcastle the following day. That Brierley knew Steel – a former Glasgow Wheeler himself of course – was all the incentive Fairweather needed to join the Wheelers, treating himself to a new Flying Scot with wages from his new job on the Clyde.

The still-junior Fairweather made rapid progress, winning his first race, a novice-only '25' time trial in which he broke the record but "I'm too embarrassed to to tell you my time!" The following year he found himself at the Commonwealth and Empire Games in Cardiff, riding the kilo on the track, his last serious foray on the boards as after that he concentrated on racing on the roads.

Fairweather was selected for the Scottish team in the 1961 Tour of Britain and before the start targeted stage thirteen's brutal hike over the Pennines into Morecambe as 'his' stage. Not only did Fairweather win that stage, but Scotland won the team prize that day too. Steel had visited the stage start at Buxton two days earlier. "Too bad he hadn't come up to Morecambe," laughs Fairweather, who was on fine form. "I don't know what was in that water, but I was sorry I couldn't bring a barrel back up the road with me!"

Fairweather's form earned him selection for the Great Britain team that was headed for the Tour of East Germany. "A big mistake. That was the weekend they closed the border!" Sure enough, amid rising tensions in the four sectors of post-war Germany, in late May 1961 the Soviet Union closed the borders. "There were tanks and armed guards all over the place," recalls Fairweather, "a couple of the guys selected never even turned up, thinking they wouldn't get back out."

Back on home soil – or almost – Fairweather was back racing in the Milk Race the following spring. Still only 22, it was to be a turning point in Fairweather's international riding career. Alfie needed a result to get selection for the 1962 Commonwealth and Empire Games in Perth, Australia, so was well motivated. Having finished second on one stage – and just missed the yellow jersey that would have come with the time bonus – Fairweather hit the deck in a high-speed crash four stages from the finish. "I got back on the bike and finished, but that night I was in a lot of pain and I had a lump in my groin. I started and finished the next day's stage in agony. The stage after that was the same one |I had won in 1961 and, although I took the start, I packed after just a few miles."

Thinking that his chances of Scottish Games selection had gone, Fairweather was surprised to find himself named as one of two riders on the Scottish road team – there was, apparently, only enough funding for two riders out of a possible four places available. The other slot went to Ian Thomson of the VC Stella, a future Scottish team manager.

Fairweather and Thomson found themselves chasing wheels all day. "The Australians, English, New Zealanders and Canadians seemed to have riders in every break. So we would chase and then riders would attack over the top of us. That was it, I had nothing left and just rode into the finish. When I crossed the line I said to myself 'That's it, I'm never going to race again.' To crown it all off I was put down as a 'DNF' in the official results. I didn't race again for 12 years, I took 12 years off."

Much later, results were amended to show that Fairweather actually finished 19th in a race won by future pro, Englishman Wes Mason. International adventures aside, Fairweather was club road race champion three seasons on the trot from 1958 to 1961.

If Alfie had 'spat the dummy' after the disappointment of the 1962 Commonwealth Games, deep down, he was still a bike rider, still a Glasgow Wheeler at heart. "For a while my Saturday's were me sitting in an armchair with four bottles of beer at my side, watching the 'Black and white minstrels' on the TV. Then one night I said to myself 'There must be something better for me in this life.' So I decided to get the bike out."

Ironically it was a Johnstone Wheelers club-confined '10' on the Georgetown flats that got Fairweather back in the saddle with a number pinned to his jersey. "I only had the miles in my legs from cycling to work, but I said to myself that if I finish within a minute of the winner I would start training and racing again. I finished 45 seconds down on the winner, but that was it. And, by the way, it was the first, last and only time the winner that night beat me!"

Sure enough, Fairweather buckled down and got back to training, winning the first '25' of his comeback season as well as the winning the club's time trial championship. It was a position that Fairweather would hold for the next decade. As a veteran Fairweather took the start in twenty-nine '25' mile time trials, winning 12 and finishing as runner up in the other 17. "I was always beaten by the same guy – Dave Hannah of the Regent – who was Scottish '25' champion and record holder. He was also half my age! I did manage one victory over him and he was the first to come over and congratulate me."

If the early 1960s had been Fairweather's peak road racing years, once his comeback was underway, he excelled in longer time trial distances. However, arguably the finest late career moment was winning the British veteran (when the category was open to all riders over 40) road race title on the Isle of Man in 1981. He had finished on the third step of the podium in 1979 on the same course, so he knew his way around the island by then. "I turned to Alan (son) who was there when I got off the podium and said, if the race is here again I'll win it." Sure enough, Fairweather did just that, attacking the break on a drag, dropping pre-race favourites Bill Painter and Brian Rourke to take a solo victory. "I don't think I have ever won an easier race," he recalls.

For good measure Fairweather won the Scottish vets title the following season. In 1984 Fairweather was still racing, and won the Glasgow Road Club organised 100 mile time trial title aged 46. Fairweather and his son Alan were prominent and active racing members of the club until 1985 when the family emigrated to Ontario in Canada, though at the time of writing, in 2023, Alfie still considered himself "a Wheeler at heart."

Back when Alfie Fairweather started riding and racing on Scotland's roads, he was fortunate to do so at a point when the roads were still quiet and relatively car-free. However, as the 1950s wore on and increased affluence meant people had more money to spend, there turned out to be a downside for cycling. The car became affordable, which was to have a profound impact on British culture, town planning and civil engineering projects in the following decades.

It's a curious fact that when the British Cycling Federation emerged to unite cycling's factions, that cycling was actually starting to dip, nationally. In 1959, at the first BCF annual general meeting, the hot topic was membership decline. And this wasn't some doom-monger trying to scare the new organisation into action, it was recognised as a serious issue. The slump was "likely to continue unless everybody interested in the sport and pastime of cycling does their best to spread its popularity." Alongside the rise in car ownership came a hike in road haulage traffic. 1955 saw the arrival of the 'juggernauts' when 24-tonne laden lorries were permitted on the roads for the first time. There were 5,000 of such lorries in 1955. By 1970 the lorries pounding our roads – now 32 tonne articulated behemoths – numbered 55,000.

Cyclists – of all kinds – were getting squeezed off the roads. To put things in context, in the late 1940s cycling was second only to the bus when it came to getting to work, accounting for one-fifth of all commuting journeys in 1949. However, between 1950 to 1970, car ownership in the UK increased *five-fold*. The roads were getting busier, much busier. The inter-war and immediate post-war years had seen cycling's popularity peak and from here on, the car would begin to dominate town, road and civil engineering planning for the next 70 years. Car culture and all the decisions that flowed from it, was in the ascendancy.

In a parallel though related two-wheeled world, the Cyclists Touring Club (CTC) post-War membership had peaked in 1950 at 53,574, thence starting a slow downward trend that had set off the same alarm bells inside the BCF and SCU at the end of that decade. The rise of the car had seen cycling slip from the mainstream, both as a means of transport and as a sport. Not that anyone realised this at the time, but cycling was on the way to becoming the niche sport and activity it would remain in Scotland for the next 60 years.

As Fairweather accrued results in the senior ranks, 1962 saw the entry of promising junior Billy Bilsland, whose father Alec had been in the club 25 years earlier and had been a member of the Scottish two-mile team pursuit championship winning quartet in 1939. Bilsland and his brothers were all members of the Wheelers, but their best days still lay a few years ahead. And in reaching those better days and results would in part be down to another Wheeler based in the north eastern edge of Glasgow, coach Jimmy Dorward.

Dorward, a coach of some repute – both for his efficacy and fearsome reputation as a disciplinarian – had been the *de facto* coach at the Wheelers for several years. Dorward had been a member of the West of Scotland Clarion before a certain 'Jim Dorward' from Springburn joined the Wheelers in 1950 gaining a reputation for innovation when it came to coaching theory and practice.

Dorward was among the first Scottish cycling coaches to introduce '*fartlek*' sessions to riders, a Swedish word meaning 'speed play' which involved unstructured training sessions – full pelt up hills, fast pedalling in low gears, dawdling, random sprint efforts of different durations, all designed to stress specific cycling skills, but keeping it entertaining. Much less entertaining were Dorward's interval sessions 'Round the graveyard' wherein Dorward sent his riders around a triangular 'loop' that took in part of the Kirkintilloch road and around Cadder cemetery. Dorward would time these efforts and the reward for maintaining a strong series of repetitions would be his gnomic 'Aye, you were moving well.' Dorward would run several riders around the 'triangle' during the same session and he would happily play one rider off another, conveniently 'forgetting' to check his various stopwatches if a rider needed a boost or a brickbat. Dorward had his preferred riders and many will insist he had a cruel streak and a tendency to favour particular riders to a near sadistic extent. Notwithstanding those facts, many were the Glasgow Wheelers who endured those graveyard intervals, because their impact was beyond doubt. Even through on the East coast, Scottish international, Commonwealth Games rider (and future national coach) Sandy Gilchrist had heard of the 'Cemetery' sessions. "We used to wonder what the hell was going on when guys talked about 'going round the cemetery' what was it? Back then, in the late 1960s and very early 1970s, training was basically riding your bike. That was it, you just rode your bike, but Jimmy introduced a lot of new ideas, he was way ahead of his time in many ways, he was a real innovator. Nobody knew about fartlek training then, it just didn't fit in with what was going on at the time." Dorward was in fact a member of the British Association of Sports and Medicine as early as February 1968.

Dorward's most successful protege had made his first appearance in the Membership book in the 1961-62 season, a 16-year-old listed as 'William Bilsland' from Milton, a neighbour of the venerable Jimmy Brinkins, both living in the shadow of the Campsie hills and the famous Crow road climb.

Dorward would have a hand in coaching Bilsland, Sandy Gordon, Robert Millar, Jamie McGahan and Mike Lawson but left the club in 1974 to set up the Scotia CC, his intention being to attract and develop young talent. It was a shock move, a move that some in the club never *completely* forgave, including Bilsland, yet a measure of the esteem that Dorward was held in the club that when he formed the Scotia he wasn't 'drummed out,' given that he 'took' a number of promising young Wheelers with him, including young Lawson.

Dorward, who had been a draughtsman at John Brown Shipyard on the Upper Clyde, had briefly managed Scottish international teams in the 1970s and his clashes with what is still called 'the Establishment' were legendary. Reflecting on the reasons for friction, Gilchrist, a Scottish international of the era, reflects that Dorward was perhaps too much of an innovator. "Back then, you had a national team manager – Ian Thomson (of the Ivy CC) who would make selections and take teams away. But he had to get his choices ratified by the Racing Committee of the Scottish Cyclists Union (SCU) and I think they were a lot more 'old school' than Jimmy in a lot of ways, so if Jimmy had new ideas he believed in, there was always the chance of some friction."

It was, almost invariably, 'My way or the highway' with Dorward and he was a hard task master who expected total commitment from the riders under his watch. Dorward gave enormous amounts of time and energy to the club and its riders and if he felt that a rider wasn't reciprocating, he wouldn't be shy in calling a rider out in public.

Yet, for all his spiky reputation, when measured against the results of his riders, he was the best coach in Scotland and he gave his time as freely to lowly third category racers as he did to the international elite. His death on 24 August 2012, aged 87, provoked an outpouring of affectionate, generous memories from the riders in many different clubs he had helped throughout the previous half century.

If the Glasgow Wheelers produced some of Scotland's finest road riders, that was in no small part down to the fact that the biggest, best and hardest races were on the west side of the country. From the grippy David Bell Memorial organised by the Ayr Roads CC over the Carrick hills, the Sam Robinson Memorial around the Trossachs (from 1975, won by Jamie McGahan in 1979), the Drummond

Trophy on a hilly Cathkin-East Kilbride circuit, the west had the road events.

But, if the west had long been the best in Scotland when it came to road racing, everyone knew that continental Europe – France and Belgium in particular – was where the very best bike racing was. For any ambitious British rider, that was where you had to go to really prove yourself. Billy Bilsland was not minded to rest on his laurels and finishing his apprenticeship in joinery could wait. While today's gilded youth enjoy plane tickets, fast cars and personal managers, press officer-curated websites, instant mobile access to anyone, anywhere in the world, Bilsland raced in Belgium in 1964 where a flight to Oostende from Abbotsinch (now renamed Glasgow International) airport cost £26. They flew in a Douglas Dakota twin-prop plane. What with email being over thirty years from being invented, when 18-year-old Bilsland and his fellow travellers went from Glasgow to Gent they entered a Twilight zone, living on prize money won in Menin, Kortijk, Ingelmunster, Roeselare and anywhere else they lined up. The competition was fierce, of course, and locals didn't appreciate Scots coming over and trying to earn a slice of prize money. Not only did you need bike handling skills and physical talent, you needed the appropriate attitude and there was nowhere like the Belgian race circuit to teach you what it took.

Coming back to race for Scotland in the 1966 Tour of Scotland Milk Race, Bilsland won stage four's 140 mile romp from Largs to Dunbar – and Bilsland was just 20 years old. As Andy McGhee, a Glasgow rival on the same Scotland team put it, "Billy was a great guy and we got on well – but put him on a bike and he'd cut your throat!" In the road race bunch, the law of the jungle prevailed.

During the Peace Race in 1967, Bilsland was in a two-rider break coming onto a cinder track in Liberec sports stadium. "I was away with a big Russian and, as we went into the tunnel to get into the stadium, I hooked him and went on to win the stage. After the presentation he came striding towards me and I thought I was in big trouble, but he just stuck his hand out to shake mine." There are some things they don't teach you, not even in a Jimmy Dorward coaching session...

The fact that Bilsland made it to Mexico in 1968 at the age of 22 was a measure of his talent and also his ambition. Realising that if he wanted to gain selection he would have to put himself in front of the GB selectors and race against the best, he had to move south. Like Jackie Bone 20 years earlier, Bilsland packed his bags – and his tools – and headed south, ending up in Handsworth, a suburb of Birmingham (or Aston, to be precise).

Bilsland was working as a finishing joiner in a local estate, staying in digs with a landlady, training and racing. "I would work some days till lunchtime, then go out training, finish up, have a shower, then go back to work at night, because the site had night watchmen and security. I was earning good money and in the end my foreman had a word to tell me to calm down."

Unorthodox preparation aside, Bilsland raced as a Glasgow Wheeler and, with the benefit of 50 years of hindsight, reckons he made one mistake. "I should have joined the Coventry CC, I should never have raced as a Wheeler, that jersey was too easy to spot! Plus, any time I went up the road, they chased. If I had had some team mates maybe I would have won more!" In the end, Bilsland won enough to get his ticket to the high altitude Games of Mexico City in 1968.

"Five of us went but only four were going to ride the road race. You know how they selected the final four? Three days before the race, we went out behind a motorbike – at altitude of course – and the first guy to get dropped wasn't going to get selected. So we were riding up this hill just about flat-out, lined out behind the bike and I was tucked in right behind it, first in line. Suddenly I see Dave Rollinson's front wheel coming up on my left and I knew if I let him push me out I would be off the back. But...you know that old adage? That a pedal in the front wheel is a good deterrent? Well, he got the message. In the end poor John Bettinson got blown away and didn't make the team. Funnily enough in the official record, the fourth man is recorded as Bettinson. Bettinson never spoke to me again, which was a shame, because I got on well with him, but that's the way they selected the team for the Games. To be honest we never really saw Maurice Cumberworth, who was meant to be managing the team.

He was there with his girlfriend, so we never saw him – that's true!" chuckles Bilsland.

Bilsland turned pro with Peugeot in 1970 – just three years after Peugeot's Tommy Simpson had died on Mont Ventoux – with a *carte de visite* that was peppered with impressive British, French and international results as well as a selection for the 1968 Olympic Games road race in Mexico.

Bilsland would marry Isla Campbell, the daughter of Arthur, fellow Wheeler, president of the Scottish Cyclists' Union and BCF board member, team manager in the 1963 Peace Race (amongst other races) and, eventually, a UCI International Commissaire. Campbell was chief commissaire at the 1980 world road championships in Sallanches, when Bernard Hinault won the title (and Robert Millar was fourth). Few cycling people in Scotland were as well connected as Campbell – though one of his protégés, Gerry McDaid would forge his own path as as UCI international commissaire, working, famously, as the medical inspector on the 1989 Tour de France.

Campbell was a stickler for the rule book and his understanding of what was and was not permissible within the framework of rules, points of order and regulations was terrifying in its detail. Your club delegation might have a fantastic point to make, but if it hadn't been minuted or broke some point of order, Campbell would be quick to rule it 'out of order' and therefore inadmissible. If you went into battle with Arthur Campbell, you better know the rules of engagement – because Arthur knew them in at least two languages.

Recognised by friends, rivals and enemies as a consummate politician, Campbell was not above the darker arts, as this anecdote reveals.

When Bilsland was establishing his shop in the Saltmarket, the rookie retailer was making contacts with various suppliers and, among them, was Campagnolo in Italy. Throughout the 1970s, Campagnolo was simply the only name in town when it came to racing components. Of course there were other (French and German) brands, but every rider aspired to Campagnolo.

However, Italy being Italy, it wasn't always easy to communicate or negotiate, particularly during *'Ferragosto'* when the whole of Italy went on holiday. To cut a long story short, Billy felt he was getting fobbed off by Campagnolo, struggling to get an account up and running with the Vicenza factory. When Bilsland finally *did* manage to get through to Italy he was informed that 'Nobody had time to talk with him at the moment.'

At the world track championships later that year, it just so happened that the UCI had appointed Arthur Campbell to be Chief Commissaire and, ever a stickler for even the smallest print in the regulations, noted that the track side banners of one particular sponsor were not quite the regular size or position. Following the rules to the letter, Campbell had them taken down before the start of the opening day.

Campagnolo – yes, it was their banners, what were the chances? – representatives were outraged and demanded an explanation from Campbell who, regretfully had to inform them that he didn't have time to speak to them at that precise moment. Is it any wonder that so many riders were happy to have Arthur Campbell on their side?

Jack Fancourt wins the controversial Isle of Man road race in 1937 ahead of Glasgow Wheelers duo Jackie Bone and Donald Morrison.

A smiling Alex Hendry and Arthur Campbell (behind) with a more pensive Wheeler before a Glasgow road race start from George Square in 1947.

Pat McCabe, a keen photographer as well as a lifelong Wheeler, who joined the club in 1930 and remained a member for life.

Joe Patterson, a Wheelers fixture on committees and club runs, Patterson was another stalwart who first joined the club in 1946.

Ex-Wheeler George Edwards (left) and friend 'photo bomb' the Wheelers team at the start of the 1946 Tour of Britain. Stewart Montgomery, Jimmy Brown link arms with Alex Hendry and Arthur Campbell on the right.

At the finish of the 1951 Tour of Britain at Helenvale cinder track. Alec Hutchison, John Glass and John Thayne with fellow Wheelers 'Zeke' Walker and a young Jimmy Parker looking on.

Dougie Hamilton in a 1958 cyclo-cross race on a steel-framed single-speed. Never let it be said that the Wheelers weren't hipsters...

Every one a racer. A Wheelers shot from 1960. From the left: Dougie Hamilton, John Thayne, Jimmy Calder, Alex Logan, Alex Calder, Robert Thayne and Alec 'Eck' Hutchison.

John Thayne helped keep the club afloat through some bleak seasons, but he still raced, seen here at on the Dukes Pass at the Tour of the Trossachs time trial.

A 22-year-old Billy Bilsland (in a Scotland top) wins stage 13 of the 1967 Peace Race in the Czech city of Liberec.

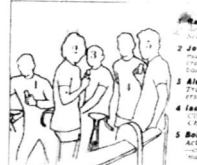

Marsgate. The 'controversial' 1966 advert featuring (left to right) Rab Campbell, Johan Thayne, Alec Calder, Ian Gardner and Bob Macauley on the Dukes Pass.

Still only 19, Billy Bilsland, riding for Scotland, wins his second stage at the Tour of Slovakia in 1965 ahead of a Czech and East German. He led the race overall for three days.

Aside from his politicking, Arthur Campbell did several spells as a team manager too, as here at the Peace Race in 1964, making contacts that would serve him well later in his career at the UCI.

Stage 17 podium of the 1985 Tour of Spain. Pello-Ruiz Cabestany (right) won the time trial, but third-placed Robert Millar took the race lead. Next day a dubious coalition of Spanish riders – and the misjudgment of Peugeot directeur sportif Roland Berland – trapped Millar and he would end up second overall, 36 second behind Pedro Delgado.

Millar and Campbell before the start of the 1988 Kellogg's Tour of Britain in Newcastle.

Mike Lawson leads Tom Anderson in the 1987 Scottish national road race. He finished fifth behind winner Finlay Gentleman in Fife.

Neil MacLeod 'smiling' in the mountain time trial stage of the 1989 Tour of Speyside.

Neah Evans, a Glasgow Wheeler for a few short seasons, racing in Belgium prior to the 2014 Commonwealth Games in Glasgow.

5

GLASGOW'S SWINGING SIXTIES

AFTER TWO GRIM post-war decades of rebuilding and rationing, Britain finally picked itself up and pressed on. Throughout the 1950s the economy gathered steam, the 'baby boomers' got busy and cycling stretched its legs. Some Sunday papers now came with colour supplements and in all walks of life it was as if the lights had been turned on again.

Following its (re)formation in 1952, the Scottish Cyclists' Union had wasted little time in expanding its field of operations and consolidating the sport as best it could. It was still running on a miniscule budget and steered by volunteers, from top to bottom. By the mid-1960s there were 74 clubs affiliated to the SCU comprising approximately 800 members. In a newspaper cutting from 1967, the financial accounts are laid bare. "The shoestring yearly income of the controlling SCU, which operates efficiently without any Government grants, is between £500 and £600 yearly and this year £560."

By way of modern comparison, in 2022, Scottish Cycling (SC) had 174 clubs and 1,318 licence holders, in categories from elite to under-12 youth. Given that there were almost 600 youth and under-12 licences and recalling that this total also included those who raced mountain bikes, it's clear that cycling's profile has changed considerably.

It's worth noting too that in 2022 SC received government grants of £900,000, had a turnover of £2.7 million and now employs around 50 staff at the Sir Chris Hoy velodrome. All things considered – staff, resources, communications, facilities – you have to say that those 1960s volunteers were doing a decent job.

Back in 1967, that *Evening Times* article also noted that "Scottish chairman Arthur Campbell is a British delegate to the UCI. He is also on the international jury which adjudicates on world class races. This is a rare honour." It was indeed a rare honour and there weren't many Scots who would make it all the way to a seat at the table of the Executive Committee of the UCI.

In the mid-1960s the SCU may not have had much money in the bank, but it was enthusiastic and well connected and had still managed to organise a Tour of Scotland, first run in 1955. Once again, there were Wheelers involved both on the road and in the back rooms. The 1958 edition of the Tour of Scotland – backed by the Scottish Daily Express no less, piggy-backing on the Daily Express' sponsorship of the Tour of Britain – was a three day event whose organising committee comprised Hughie Boyd of the Glenmarnock Wheelers and Campbell.

For good measure, Campbell was also the Chief Commissaire on the race, while other Wheelers were involved too: Joe Patterson organised registrations, the timekeeper was Alex Calder and the recorder a certain John Thayne. Alex Logan was riding for a Glasgow composite team, so that year at least the club was better represented behind the scenes than on the road.

As the 1960s unwound, if it seemed that there was a new spirit in the land, possibly because there was. While there's much bogus rose-tinted nostalgia about the 'good old days,' by most useful measures the UK in the later 1950s and 1960s saw significant improvements in the lives of its citizens.

For some wider context, gross domestic product (GDP) in the UK more than doubled between 1955 and 1973 and household disposable income almost doubled between 1955 and 1975 too, from £1,200 to £2,200. There was – crudely – more money in the Scottish economy and there were more pounds in people's pockets than there had been for decades. There was more food and a growing variety of consumer goods in the shops too.

Compulsory National Service came to an end in 1963, the Beatles released 'She loves you' that same year, teenagers started being teenagers and, in the words of poet Philip Larkin, 'Sexual intercourse began/ in nineteen sixty-three (which was rather late for me)/ Between the end of the "Chatterley" ban/ And the Beatles first LP.' That other 'poet' of the era, Bob Dylan, wasn't kidding when he wrote 'the times they are a-changin'. There was work, there was money, people were buying cars – some from Arthur Campbell on Duke street – and the Glasgow Wheelers were ready to travel.

Thus the Wheelers' East Kilbride-based duo Hector Thomson and Rab Dewar would make their way to Belgium for a summer of racing in 1960. Basing themselves in the heart of the West Flemish magic in Kortrijk, they were aided and abetted by a revolving band of Glasgow riders from the the Ivy, the Nightingale and Suburban CC. Later that season, Thomson made the most of his Belgian experience by coming back for the 1960 national road race championship and winning it at the age of 24. Thomson hadn't won too much prior to heading to Flanders, but in the hurly-burly of the Belgian *kermis* circuit, the slightly-built Thomson learned his trade – because he had to! If you didn't win some primes at least, your cupboard would remain empty, your rations limited.

The following season Thomson was selected to ride the Milk Race won by English Olympian Billy Holmes. Thomson was part of a Scotland team that also included fellow Wheeler Alfie Fairweather (18th overall at 23-years-old) as well as future Scottish national team manager Ian Thomson and Glenmarnock stalwart Norrie 'Drummond Trophy' Drummond. Gloriously, Fairweather won the stage into Morecambe, while experienced Hughie McGuire bagged two stages en route to a fine fifth overall.

Next, in 1962 Thomson would finish 39th riding in a 'Commonwealth' team in that year's thirteen-stage Milk Race. The team also featured his fellow Wheeler and East Kilbride training partner Rab Dewar, who would arrive in Weston-super-Mare in 19th place overall. Thomson married in 1965 and emigrated to Canada, which put an end to his Scottish racing career.

Thomson competed a little in Canada – where he found himself surrounded by wily Italian ex-pats – but returned to Scotland in 1973 and was a key player in the re-formation of the East Kilbride Wheelers in 1982 with Willie Inches, yet another former Wheeler living in East Kilbride. By then the only club in the new town was the St Christopher's CC and, considering it to be more of a time trialling club, Thomson and Inches decided a road racing oriented outfit was required. At which point, the pair revitalised the dormant East Kilbride Wheelers.

Hard as it may be to imagine from a millennial perspective, but in the 1960s, club life included all sorts of riders and all levels of aptitude. Which is to say that in the modern era, in the 2020s, when racing became more specialised, club life can seem archaic and quaint.

In the 1960s, a Sunday club run would include internationals, veterans, newcomers and third cats, and 'drum-ups' were more important than cafe stops being both cheaper and easier. There weren't so many posh wee cafes dotted around rural Scotland in the 1960s and a troop of soggy cyclists would hardly be made welcome in a genteel tea room. Not forgetting of course that in 1960s Scotland, almost everything was shut on a Sunday club run anyway!

Thus, after a summer of racing, the top senior riders in the club would be out on winter club runs, brewing tea and heating up soup at the drum-up spots in Fintry, the Carron Valley, Loch Lomond, Beith loch or the Lake of Menteith to name a very few. These spots were all well-known to Glasgow clubs and, if permissions to start tea-making fires were not actively sought, they were tolerated. According to one account from the era, Rab Dewar spotted a dead salmon in the bottom of a pool beside a river, howked it out and proceeded to gut and cook it. It's a long, long way from a foil tube of caffeine and glucose polymer gel.

Speaking, as we are, of 'race food' then 1966 saw a curious tale involving what once constituted a key element in every club rider's ride food – the Mars bar. Bizarrely, the Glasgow Wheelers became involved in what today would probably be called 'Marsgate.' In

1966 there was still, in terms of regulations, a very clear distinction between amateur and professional, between grubby sponsorship and Corinthian purity. That year, for reasons best known to the Mars marketing department in London, the Glasgow Wheelers were selected to front a print advertising campaign for the famous Mars bar.

The ad featured "five stalwarts of a thriving cycling club, Glasgow Wheelers," Rab Campbell, Johan Thayne, Alex Calder, Ian Gardner and Bob Macauley. The smiling quintet were photographed in club jerseys clutching Mars bars overlooking Aberfoyle. The advert insisted that 'Mars bars make the going easy' and in the mid-1960s, before the arrival of glucose polymers, gels and fructose-glucose drinks, few cyclists would have disagreed. Who among us had never scoffed a Mars bar in our moment of greatest nutritional need?

The ad created a 'storm' in Scottish cycling circles since some claimed it was in contravention of sponsorship guidelines or the amateur spirit or some other arcane regulation. The club knew all along that it was skating on thin ice. When first contacted by Mars, the club committee recorded that "There was a careful examination of the amateur definition to see if the proposed action contravenes the regulation, but it was felt that there was no infringement."

The club duly changed the destination of a Sunday run on 27 February and the agency photographer posed the five riders on the Dukes pass, Mars bars in hand. After which Alex Calder was handed a cheque for £25 as a 'modelling fee.'

Though the story cannot be confirmed, rumour has it that the Johnstone Wheelers were behind a subsequent complaint made to the SCU executive committee, demanding that a letter of censure be sent to the club. Things took a turn for the worse as the SCU demanded the advert be withdrawn and the club responded by asking the BCF precisely which rules had been broken.

All of which was moot, when one of the 'models,' Ian Gardner, died while racing a '25' on the Kippen flats after hitting a truck. The club then requested that the advert be withdrawn by Mars, which it duly did. Unfathomably, given the circumstances, the SCU and BCF pursued the matter. The club, in the shape of Jimmy Dorward and

Alex Calder then sought legal advice ahead of an anticipated stramash at the year end SCU Annual General Meeting. The lawyer declared the club was in the right and, at the following AGM, the issue was never mentioned.

Inside the club in the early 1960s, were two young riders who were pushing each other hard and making names for themselves at home and abroad. Both were from Glasgow, one had a longer history at the club than the other, but both would win every road race worth the effort in Scotland. From the Sam Robinson memorial around the Trossachs to the Davie Bell memorial in the hills behind Girvan to the national road race, the Tour of the Trossachs time trial and the national '25' time trial and many others besides. Between them, Billy Bilsland and Sandy Gordon won whatever was worth winning in Scotland at the time.

Both had raced as juniors, albeit Gordon was in the West of Scotland Clarion at the time. When Gordon joined the Wheelers as a first year senior, he and Bilsland formed a formidable duo, though to call them a 'team' might have been stretching it a bit. It would be accurate to say that having two massively talented and ambitious riders in the same jersey generated some friction.

To give a flavour of their racing relationship, one 'Billy and Sandy' anecdote will probably suffice. At a road race on Barrhead circuit the two Wheelers had broken clear and were well ahead of the chasers – a two-up sprint would decide the outcome. Under normal circumstances, Gordon, with his track experience, was the faster finisher. Bilsland was surely going to finish second...

...unless of course he decided to guide Gordon up onto the pavement in the hectic sprint for the line. Nudged towards the kerb at 30mph by Bilsland's shoulder, Gordon retaliated, reached out and pushed Bilsland. The race commissaires promptly disqualified them both.

Both Bilsland and Gordon had made their talents known even as junior riders and when they turned senior, the 'old order' was turned upside down. In the late 1950s and early years of the 1960s, the strongest team in Scotland had been the VC Stella, a prototype 'race team' to which you had to be invited to join. Two-time Scottish national road champion Ernie Scally, winner of the 1957 Tour of Scotland (and 1961 Tour de France rider) Kenny Laidlaw, Scottish national team manager from 1970-90 Ian Thomson and Ronnie Park were the top men of the day. They were the undisputed big hitters until Bilsland and Gordon turned up to ruffle feathers other than each others.

Bilsland recalls that, as a junior, the riders in the VC Stella were among those who he aspired to compete against and, in short order, he did just that.

Like riders he would mentor in later decades, Bilsland's talent was clear from an early stage. In 1963, working as an apprentice joiner in Glasgow, one of his work colleagues was also a cyclist and the two of them crammed bikes into the boot and drove up to the Scottish National '25' championship where Bilsland, still a junior, was unseeded. "My pal went for a warm up and came back to the car and he said, 'I've just seen the winner, John Ritchie - he's a guy who doesn't even break sweat,' and I nodded. But I went out and did a '58' (in fact a 58-11, a personal best) and won by 11 seconds," smiles Bilsland, recalling the day 60 years later. There's a twinkle in the eye and a faint smile at the memory. Needless to say, Bilsland was the Junior best all-rounder time trial champion in Scotland that year too.

Bilsland was dedicated and enthusiastic, his passion stoked by reading about European Tours and Classics in *International Cycle sport* magazine and coming from a family – father and brothers – that were sporting enthusiasts. Basically, Bilsland wanted to be a professional bike rider and set out to do just that. Still just 17-years-old in the summer of 1964 he headed to Kortijk in west Flanders for the summer to ride for the TV Prisma to hone his race skills in the hurly-burly of Belgian amateur racing. There were primes won and bouquets of flowers and a race win in the shadow of the famous Menin gate. Bilsland's appetite was whetted, his ambitions further stoked. On his return to Scotland, his relationship with his coach Jimmy Dorward moved up a notch.

As a 19-year-old he won the Glasgow-Dunoon classic with an audacious solo raid that saw him win by almost two minutes before the rest of the field arrived, led in by club mate and arch rival Sandy

Gordon who, like Bilsland, was being coached by Dorward. The rivalry between the two riders was growing and the fact that they had the same coach only added to the friction.

That same year, 1966, four years after he joined the club as a junior, the 20-year-old Bilsland was on his way to the Commonwealth Games in Jamaica to represent Scotland in the road race. He finished ninth behind Peter Buckley from the Isle of Man, but came back and won the Tour of the Trossachs, which was some small consolation. He repeated the feat the following year in foul wintery conditions, handing out a near four-minute beating to the second placed rider Peter Robertson and claiming the Dukes pass hill climb prime to boot. Bilsland was still barely 21-years-old.

For his part, 1966 had been a big year for Gordon too, albeit for very different reasons and his absence from the results in the Trossachs wasn't a surprise, considering that he had been in a coma earlier that summer. While racing in the Tour of Austria as part of a Great Britain team, Gordon rode into a stationary car coming off a fast descent. It was a horrific crash that almost cost him his life.

"Apparently I was loaded onto a truck being used as an ambulance," explained Gordon many years later. The medical provision at international stage racing having improved considerably in the intervening years. "I had severe head injuries, my nose was broken and I had countless cuts on my arms and legs. We set off for a hospital near Vienna and it seems the ambulancemen took their eyes off me for a moment and in that brief time I swallowed my tongue." Gordon's heart stopped briefly and he remained unconscious for eight days, his condition so serious that the Wheelers paid for his mum's plane ticket so she could be by his bedside. Gordon survived and, in time, returned to racing.

It's clear that Gordon and Bilsland were both extremely talented, yet in the end it was Bilsland who pressed ahead. Perhaps, in the end, it boiled down to talent – that unquantifiable mix of physiology, mental toughness and desire? When asked if he ever thought about a pro career in England or the continent Gordon replied, "Not in England, no. I remember in 1965 Billy and I went to Belgium to race on our holidays for three weeks. We finished a six hour Milk Race stage on the Saturday, travelled to Belgium on the Sunday and rode a 100 kilometre *kermis* on the pave in the wet on the Monday – I could hardly move after it. My best placing was 11th on that trip – there was no messing, if you were in the break then you went through or ended up in the ditch. It was very hard racing but you would have adapted to it if you were living there. When Billy went to France I remember my mother saying that I had a good job, why throw it in? And how many guys really make it over there?"

In 1967 – when Bilsland was 21 and Gordon 20 – Dorward decided to end his coaching relationship with both riders. He decided to "part company" from the point of view of training because "they had only been prepared to keep to (training) schedules and ask for advice when form was dropping off." As ever with Jimmy Dorward, it was his way or no way. Dorward then became a coach to anyone who wanted to follow him, though of course he would form the Scotia CC in Bishopbriggs in 1974.

Nearer the end of the decade, in 1968, for the first time since 1936, a Glasgow Wheeler was back at the Olympic Games. In the decades since Jackie Bone had been selected to race in that inaugural Berlin Olympic road race, the sport had grown in popularity, bikes now had derailleur gears and, globally, the sport was starting to assume uniform rules as national federations became established and affiliated themselves to the UCI.

In the run-up to the Games Bilsland finished second behind another Olympian – John Bettinson – in the Manx International road race, albeit he was racing in the blue of Scotland.

Thus, the road race in Mexico City featured 'William Law Bilsland' riding for the Great Britain team managed by Maurice Cumberworth. The other riders were Dave Rollinson, Les West and Brian Jolly, with Rollinson the best finisher. Clad in a red, white and blue Great Britain jumper made from wool with pockets on the chest, Bilsland didn't finish the 196km race, but then again neither did future Tour de France winner Joop Zoetemelk, while Belgian Roger De Vlaeminck 'only' managed 18th. The race was won by one of the pre-race favourites Pierfranco Vianelli who went on to ride as one of

Eddy Merckx's mountain domestiques at the Belgian's all-conquering Molteni team.

"There wasn't a training camp or anything to help us acclimatise to the altitude or the heat," recalls Bilsland, "and we had to make our own way to London to go. I rode the 100km team time trial as well, although the other road guys didn't – and I'm not even listed as riding the time trial! Actually Les West was down to ride the team time trial but decided against it at the last minute, so he could save himself for the road race. He didn't finish it though. The teams for the two races were decided when we got to Mexico."

For the 1969 season Bilsland decided to head to France, specifically to the CSM Puteaux, a strong club based in the Paris suburbs. The biggest French clubs took part in the Merite Velo d'Or competition, a series of 28 races in which riders and clubs were awarded points for wins and placings. The individual rider who won the competition put himself in a very strong position in his search for a pro contract.

In the course of 1969 and scoring points in races like the Tour de la Sarthe, the Tour de Limousin, Paris-Ezy, Paris-Mantes, Paris-Dreux and the Ruban des Granitiers Breton, Bilsland finished third overall, behind future French star sprinter Jean-Pierre Danguillaume. In a profoundly French set-up, Bilsland was the only '*etranger*' in the top 10 of a cut-throat Merite Velo d'Or competition.

In between the Merite d'Or counting events, there was a busy calendar of events and Bilsland won his share, making headlines in French sports daily *l'Equipe*. 'My mum would go into John Smith's, the bookshop in St Vincent street, where they would get copies of it a couple of days after it came out. She'd have a look at the cycling results and if she saw my name, she'd buy a copy." Which goes some way to explaining why Bilsland's cuttings are so copious. 'Pour Bilsland, l'avarice n'est pas propre des Ecossais' was just one headline from the 1969 season. Underneath, journalist Robert Pajot noted, "A likeable guy who is always smiling, Bilsland shared the 72 bottles of wine he won with his team mates and team staff after his victory in the Paris-Saint Pourcin stage race. With that gesture he no doubt wanted to bury the reputation Scots have for being mean and miserly in so many jokes."

His prowess against the clock was also noted in other headlines. A second overall in the Tour of Nivernais-Morvan was secured with a win in the 39km time trial, ahead of his Puteaux team mate (and future pro Yves Hezard). 'L'Ecossais Bisland (sic) le meilleur contre-le-montre.' It would not be the last time the French type setters had trouble with that surname.

Given his form and results in France, Bilsland was an obvious Great Britain selection for the Tour de l'Avenir. Or, to give it its full name at the time, the Tour de France de l'Avenir – the Tour de France of the Future. The 14-stage race, run entirely in France, started in Le Mans before heading west into Brittany then winding its way down to Clermont Ferrand. There were no rest days back then and Joop Zoetemelk would triumph with the Netherlands national team. Bilsland would finish the top British rider eighth overall, only nine minutes down and – crucially – he won the penultimate 85 mile stage, the toughest of the race, in the Auvergne, at Clermont Ferrand. outsprinting his breakaway companion Zoetemelk. For his efforts in the hills of the Auvergne he ended up second in the king of the mountains but was the winner of the 'Super Amiability' prize for the most likeable rider in the race. His reward was a lot of ice cream, since the prize was sponsored by 'Miko.'

Coming out of the l'Avenir, there was the still one amateur classic to go, one more stepping stone, Paris-Tours which, at 238km was a serious undertaking and a prestigious event at the time. Active throughout the race, in the winning break, and finally winning a three-up sprint just clear of a fast-closing bunch, that Paris-Tours triumph was the cherry on top of a fine French bun.

When those French results were added to his Olympic ride, a brace of stages in the Tour of Scotland and a stage win at the ridiculously tough 1967 Peace Race, as well as his Avenir triumph, Bilsland had a strong *carte de visite* with which to advertise himself as a potential professional.

Sure enough, for 1970, he signed a contract with Peugeot alongside two other 'neo pros', Bernard Thevenet and Danguillaume who had won the Peace Race in 1969. The 25-year-old Bilsland was in very good company.

In 1970, his first pro season, he had more than decent results (10th in his first Tour of Lombardy) and riding in a high profile team, why did Bilsland's media profile lie so low? "I don't know, I really don't and at the time you don't think much about it, but I think I blotted my copybook right at the start with the editor of *Cycling Weekly* at the time, Ken Evans," muses Bilsland (and it's hard to tell if he is serious or not).

Bilsland explains that, when he as still an amateur, he had what turned out to be an unfortunate encounter with that influential English journalist. "Evans was coming back from the unveiling of the Tommy Simpson memorial on Mont Ventoux and he had hired a big Union Jack flag to drape over the memorial. He came back up to Paris and told the team manager the only reason I was riding so well was because he had me locked up so I couldn't go on a night out. And the manager, in all seriousness, turned to me and asked me if it was true! From then on the manager kept me on a very short leash. Anyway, Evans left this flag behind and asked me to post it back to him... which I didn't. And Evans was going bananas. When I say it was a flag I mean, this thing was huge, it was the size of a room – and contacted me to ask me to post it back. Well, I never got round to it. In the end he was phoning the Puteaux trying to track it down and, well, I was never there to take his call. I won Paris – Tours that year, second in Paris-Dreux, sixth in the Grand Prix des Nations and a lot of other good podiums but very little was written in the *Cycling*. Maybe I should have sent his flag straight back," observes Bilsland, with a rueful, mischievous smile.

Around the time Bilsland was leaving Glasgow and forging a career in France at CSM Puteaux, reinforcements were on the way back home, swelling club numbers and keeping the Wheelers international reputation alive. Tommy Banks' dad and older brother Albert had both been members of the Maryhill Wheelers and, inevitably, young Tommy's first club was the northside outfit. However, when Maryhill Wheelers ceased to be, in 1960, the Banks clan found themselves club-less and ended up at the Glenmarnock Wheelers. The Banks' were enthusiastic track riders, competing on the concrete oval at Grangemouth which opened in 1966, and when the track manager suggested a track-based club would be a good idea, Tommy signed up. Alas, the Grangemouth club folded in short order and Tommy opted – finally – to join the Glasgow Wheelers in the winter of 1968. "One of the attractions to me was that when I raced in England the name Glasgow Wheelers, defined where I was born and lived. The club also had a strong history and high profile at that time," adds Tommy. "I mean, where exactly was Glenmarnock or Grangemouth? But everyone knew Glasgow and it had a strong name, nationally. I knew Billy (Bilsland) and Sandy (Gordon) and they were telling me I should join." When he raced at Fallowfield in Manchester or at South Shields, they knew the Glasgow Wheelers.

It might have had a high profile in the late 1960s, but this was down to riders and club infrastructure rather than expenses being paid out. "Yes, occasionally the club would would give some assistance with expenses, but in those days virtually all were in employment, and funded themselves from their wages."

At which point, its worth pointing out that the strength of the club came from the membership rather than from sponsors, a centre of excellence or national-level coaching structures. When it came to coaching and training, riders were on their own, even when, as with Banks, they were on the verge of international selection for the Commonwealth Games. "My father was a great help to me during my cycling career, and there was a lot of stability in the Wheelers, with John Thayne in particular putting in a lot of time running the club. There were also a lot of top riders in the club, including Billy, who was great to train with, and Ian Bilsland, Sandy Gordon, Billy Munro, Phil Nunn, and the McQueen family. Jimmy Dorward was there for coaching advice too, though with Jimmy it was more about weight training. I can't say I ever really gelled with Jimmy, he was very intense."

Intense or not, the prickly Dorward was dedicated to the club and its riders. "In winter," recalls Banks, "the senior riders would go out and do a longer ride, but everyone would meet up at a pre-arranged drum-up spot. Jimmy would have led the junior and younger riders out to the spot on a shorter ride and meet up with the senior guys.

Then, after the drum, there would be a hard ride back in the road that had a bit of structure to it."

In fact, Banks reckons that the resurgence of the Wheelers in the 1960s was in part down to Dorward and his coaching methods. "I think he was the first guy to talk about 'fartlek' training – certainly he was the first person I heard talking about it. And then there were his weight training sessions in winter at Springburn sports centre, again, I think he was one of the first coaches to get riders weight training. Looking back, as a track sprinter, I should have been doing fewer reps and much higher weights, but for the road guys I'm sure it helped."

So, in between the table tennis competitions, the darts games, roller riding competitions, the pots of tea and biscuits and the passing around of copies of *Cycling Weekly* magazine, there were weights sessions. Club life and club nights, 1960s style, were important social hubs which lasted into the 1980s before dying, switching from weekly to sparsely attended monthly meets. Recall that in the 1950s and into the 1960s not every home had a phone, far less an internet-connected smart phone…

Over with Peugeot, Bilsland was making a more than decent fist of his career, often finishing as best Peugeot rider in those grippy Belgian semi-Classics where a new professional had a chance to show. In races like Het Volk (now Het Nieuwsblad), Kuurne-Brussel-Kuurne or the Scheldeprijs, Bilsland got noticed, always finishing in the top 20 and nudging the top 10. For a new professional, finishing as best Peugeot rider earned him respect. But not always money.

"I remember after the finish of the Scheldeprijs, I was in the changing room with French guys from Sonolor – one of them was future Tour de France boss Jean-Marie Leblanc – and they were talking about the *'frais de deplacement'* their expenses that the organiser paid. So I followed them and the guy said, 'Oh, but you live in Belgium, don't you?' So I got out my French *carte de sejour* from CSM Puteaux and claimed my £40!"

Earning a living as a first year professional was never going to make anyone rich, but Bilsland was doing OK. "Roughly, as a tradesman in Glasgow, you could get £20 a week, depending on the job, but my wage was £40 a week with Peugeot. And you have to remember that at the time footballers weren't getting much either. Someone like Scottish international star winger Jim Baxter was on £40 a week playing for Rangers, arguing with the club manager Scot Symon, just to insist that he should still get paid in the off season!" Those were different times for professional sportsmen, but they were changing fast.

6

BIG TIME CHARLIES

THE 1970S AND early 1980s were curious decades for the Glasgow Wheelers. On one hand, the club saw some of the greatest cycling talent Scotland had ever produced pass through its ranks. Yet at the same time, the popularity of cycling throughout Scotland was actually on the slide, after the huge spike in participation in the post-world war two era. Anecdotally – but credibly – the membership of the Scottish Cyclists' Union in the mid-1970s was around 700 souls, though the likelihood is that all would have been in clubs and the majority would race in some branch of the road sport. The Wheelers still had serious talent riding in blue and white – Sandy Gordon, Sandy Crawford, Tommy Banks, Alfie Fairweather, Jamie McGahan – but where was the new wave going to come from? A lack of fresh riding talent was not just an issue for the Wheelers. Who was going to swell the memberships of other Scottish clubs?

If the world of professional continental racing still seemed distant, difficult and unknowable, then Commonwealth Games selection was a more realistic target for ambitious Scottish riders. Given that the 1970 Games were to be held in Edinburgh, there was even more interest in the only international race that Scottish riders could 'legally' wear a Scottish jersey in.

Team selection for the 1970 'Commie Games' involved three Wheelers. On the road, Milngavie-based joiner Billy Munro should have, could have been in with a shout of a call up and a blue blazer. After all, among other things, he won the Drummond Trophy on the then brutal Cathkin Braes circuit. This was the era when 'Agony corner' was still part of the nine-mile lap (and was still in place when another Wheeler, Robert Millar, won the race with a superb solo ride eight years later).

"Well, I might have been in the running, but the team selector was Ian Thomson and he had pretty much selected the team from the previous season, so they were going down to England to race quite a bit," recalls Munro. Curiously – or perhaps unluckily – the Scottish team manager in the early part of 1969 had been Jimmy Dorward. For reasons that are lost in the mists of time (though, as ever with Dorward, we can have a good guess) Dorward fell out the Scottish cycling establishment and quit his post, at which point Arthur Campbell invited Ian Thomson to take over the reins. The former VC Stella and Ivy CC stalwart would remain in post for 20 years and six subsequent Commonwealth Games cycles.

No fewer than three Glasgow Wheelers did make the road team for the 1970 Edinburgh Games – Ian Bilsland, younger brother of Billy, was one of them. Tommy Banks was on the track sprint team, and the other was Sandy Gordon who had been racing internationally since the mid 1960s, a near contemporary and early rival of Billy. Unlike Bilsland however, Gordon opted to stay in the UK rather than take the European plunge and see if he could snag a professional contract. Instead Gordon opted for full-time employment, working for years in Yarrow shipyards on the Clyde.

Initially a member of the Glasgow Clarion, Gordon's results attracted the attention of the VC Stella but, when he heard there were no club runs or drum-ups, he declined the invite and pulled on the iconic Wheelers jersey.

At the Edinburgh Games in 1970, Gordon was instrumental in helping his Scottish team mate Brian Temple win a silver medal in the 10-mile scratch race. Temple broke clear with eventual winner Canadian Jocelyn Lovell and Trinidadian Vernon Stauble. Gordon chased down every Australian and English move that tried to bring the breakaway back or bridge across. It was, reckons Gordon, his 'best ever' ride. Given that the leading trio barely had more than half a lap of a lead, Gordon had his work cut out.

Gordon won the Scottish national road race title in 1970 (the same year as his Commonwealth Games selection) and he won it in 1972 again, just for good measure. It could be argued that Gordon's win in the 1972 road race was even more impressive than his previous triumph, considering he had ridden and won the Scottish national kilometre title on track the previous day. It was – and remains – a unique back-to-back. Winning the kilo title on the Saturday and the road race on the Sunday, a quite unthinkable feat in the current era of specialisation.

The fact is that Gordon won the road title *again* in 1975, but by then he had quit the Wheelers was racing for the Regent CC. Gordon had left the Wheelers under a cloud, having decided to go and race in the South African 'Rappoert Tour' in 1974 when the international sporting world had decided to boycott South African sport.

Interviewed by Ed Hood of the *Velo Veritas* website years later, Gordon said "It was at the time when South Africa was ostracised by sporting bodies because of the apartheid regime – but ironically there were black African guys in the race as well as Portuguese, Rhodesian and Italian squads.

"We knew the score, we'd get a two month suspension when we got back and that would be over the winter; but Arthur Campbell, who was very influential in the UCI and SCU (and honorary president of the Wheelers) – pushed for us to get a nine month ban. I didn't get back to racing until the end of June 1975 and left the Wheelers because of it." Sandy Gordon was not alone in being banned for breaking the sporting boycott by racing in that particular Rappoert Tour, with future Scottish team manager Sandy Gilchrist and Irish legend Sean Kelly also punished. Mind you, so was an Irish racer called Pat McQuaid, and he went on to become President of the UCI in 2005.

If Gordon felt that he had been hard done to – as far as he was concerned his extended ban was down to Campbell's insistence – then there were also Wheelers who felt that, if nothing else, Gordon 'owed' the club a little more loyalty. After all, when Gordon had suffered a horrific crash in the 1966 Tour of Austria riding for Great Britain, it was Wheelers money that paid for his mum to travel to the Austrian hospital where Sandy was recovering.

If Ian Bilsland and Gordon made the endurance side of the Scotland team, then Tommy Banks was the other who won the golden ticket, selected to ride the track sprint and the kilometre time trial.

Like Gordon, Banks would be racing on Meadowbank velodrome on Edinburgh's east side. It was an open-air wooden track with (by modern standards) relatively shallow banking. However, for the time, Meadowbank was about as good as it got, albeit it could have done with a roof. It might have been on the drier east coast, but it was still located in Scotland, after all.

Having said that, Banks and Gordon – as well as future generations of Scottish cyclists – were lucky that Meadowbank was built at all.

After the 1970 Commonwealth Games bid had been won by the Edinburgh pitch, the organising committee tried hard to trim costs and decided that the best track riders in the Commonwealth could race around Grangemouth's facility.

The concrete, gently-banked Grangemouth track, constructed around the outside of an athletics track, had been built in 1966, but was in no way fit to host world-class riders in an international event. Nevertheless, the Edinburgh council tried hard to ignore those who pointed this uncomfortable fact out. Even more damning was the fact that in winning the bid to host the Games in Edinburgh, the city had promised a new velodrome would be built for the Games. Once costs were considered, the Council tried back-pedalling – never easy on a track bike – and Grangemouth was earmarked for the track events. Plans for the promised state-of-the-art track that had featured in the bid document were promptly shelved.

Among those not prepared to abandon the promised new velodrome in Edinburgh was president of the Scottish Cyclists' Union, president of the British Cycling Federation, one Arthur Campbell. It just so happened that Campbell was also a UCI delegate and on the technical committee of cycling's international body. You might have thought that the councillors of Corstorphine might have thought a man with those sort of connections and experience was worth listening to. Alas...

Perhaps irked by Campbell's insistence that Grangemouth was not up to the job and that Edinburgh should indeed have to stump up for the new cycling facility it had promised, the Edinburgh City councillors decided to by-pass the SCU and go directly to the UK body, the BCF. Yes, that was the same BCF of which Campbell was also president. Edinburgh councillors liaised with the BCF Secretary to try to get UCI approval for Grangemouth.

Unsurprisingly, Campbell was kept appraised of developments and when the UCI track racing delegation arrived at Edinburgh airport to travel to Grangemouth, they asked where Campbell was and why he wasn't part of the delegation. Just for good measure they added that there was no way any decision could be taken by the UCI unless Campbell – a member of its technical delegation after all – was directly implicated. Bluntly, it was explained that either Arthur was involved or the Italian UCI representative was on the next plane back home.

As it turned out – and to the surprise of *nobody* who understood international-standard velodrome requirements – the UCI decreed that Grangemouth was unsuitable. Tommy Banks, who had raced with his father Albert for a short-lived Grangemouth Cycling Club set up by a manager at the facility, explained. "Basically the doors from the under the stand opened right onto the back straight. Anyone walking out of those doors was stepping into the straight without any warning of who or what was on the other side. You could be racing and someone would just walk out." There was neither tunnel nor bridge to the track centre and the design of the stand in the start-finish meant it actually overhung the track – albeit slightly. "There was a catch fence that was too low as well, if you rode into it it would basically just tip you over and down a steep incline, with your feet still strapped in to your pedals," recalls Banks with a grimace.

In short, it was barely fit for a track league far less the Commonwealth Games track programme. Reluctant it may have been, but Edinburgh Corporation finally coughed up and Scotland got its brand new velodrome, an African hardwood effort designed by Schuermann Architects, the German track specialists. The track, constructed by Ron Webb from Afzelia hardwood, was reportedly held together by 860,000 nails at a final cost of £400,000.

Ironically, Campbell's championing of the Edinburgh velodrome would enable track riding domination by Edinburgh riders for decades, thanks in no small part to the City of Edinburgh Road Club and Brian Annable, but that's another book. The outdoor velodrome, in all its warped glory and giant splinters, was finally demolished in 2017.

The 250m Meadowbank velodrome and a shift from concrete to hardwood construction, wasn't the only change taking place in cycling at the time. Technology, design and materials were undergoing transformations too. The one constant in cycle sport, as true today as it was 100 years ago, is that riders are always looking for the 'new thing' that will improve their performance. That 'new thing' might be as mundane as a saddle position, perhaps 2.5mm longer cranks or a new frame design and angles. Banks was as open as any ambitious rider to new ideas.

Banks, a contemporary of Bilsland, Munro and Gordon, explains the shift. "Some guys were getting bespoke frames made, but most of the time we were guessing at seat and head angles as well as top tube lengths. So frame builders could and would build you anything, but sometimes it didn't turn out great. In the run-up to the Edinburgh Games in 1970 I was being coached by Karl Barton, who had won track sprint medals in 1958 and 1962 for England. One day we were doing a track session and, at the end, he asked if he could do a few laps on my bike. Off he went, did some laps, came off and said 'I thought I was going to die, the top tube is much too long.' And so I got a new frame with new angles and a shorter top tube. Like I said, a lot of the time there was guesswork involved!"

By the early 1970s, a British frame with Campagnolo components was considered the pinnacle by most Scottish road racers. Back then, the idea of buying a complete bike, ready-built, was unthinkable. Rather, a frame would be bought and then built up with a selection of components that the rider could afford. And not everyone could afford Campag. "On the road guys were using a Spanish brand called Zeus or BSA parts," recalls Munro, "but Campag was what we wanted."

Needless to say cost was an issue. And cost was an issue because, back in 1970, a tradesman was earning less than £20 a week. "I was working as a joiner," explains Munro, "and the last Flying Scot I bought cost me £18. That was just the frame and fork, you had to build it up from there. Roughly speaking, a lightweight steel frame would cost you about a week's wages." Munro pauses. "See, that's one of the ways cycling has changed since then. There are frames out there now that cost – what? – eight thousand pounds? More? Well, I don't know any joiners earning eight thousand a week these days," he chuckles. When Munro finally hung up his race bike in 2009 (!) he was riding an aluminium and carbon Trek with Shimano STI gears.

By the 1970s, improved travel and communications had broadened the minds of many. Italian frames were starting to trickle into the UK to accompany those sought-after Italian components from Campagnolo as well as Ambrosio, Cinelli, 3T, Galli, Modolo and Gipiemme.

Munro might still have been buying an off-the-peg frame from Rattray's, but others were looking at Italian bikes with different geometry trying to incorporate the latest styles and ideas from continental Europe.

Throughout the 1960s and 1970s, British frames were still considered world class and worth the price and effort of acquisition. British frame builders had been honing their craft for decades and several had national reputations. Unsurprisingly, some riders would go to great lengths to acquire the 'perfect' frame. Thus, the tale of a famous Glasgow Wheeler who actually rode down to London – yes, *rode* down to London – in the 1930s to collect his Hetchins frame which had extensive chrome work and, of course, those curly chainstays. "There wasn't any money for train fares," says Munro, "so Jackie Bone rode down to the Seven Sisters road in Tottenham to get the frame and swapped over the components and wheels from the bike he rode down on onto the new bike and rode it back to Glasgow."

Sixty years later custom and fashion changed, but until aluminium and then carbon frames started to dominate in the 1990s, lightweight steel frames constructed from Reynolds and Columbus tubesets were still dominant. And some brands still exerted a 'voodoo' influence on riders. No-nonsense pragmatist he may have been, but Billy Bilsland had sought out a Mercian frame because those were in vogue at the time. "Jim Hendry was briefly in the club and I remember him telling me that he had been given a frame, so…" recalls Bilsland, eyebrows raised. Credit to Billy though, he took it to David Rattray and had it resprayed and the new decals said 'Flying Scot.' Twenty years later, on his way to France the young Robert Millar had studied what bikes previous French foreign legionnaires had used. "I rode a Harry Hall (a Manchester based bike shop) because I had checked to see what frames the English guys I was racing were on. Guys like Graham Jones were on them, so that's what I wanted."

Millar (since 2017 known as Philippa York) was by far the biggest name – the best-known name – to emerge from the late 1970s. Millar finished fourth in the 1984 Tour de France and won the King of the Mountains jersey that same year, exploits which remained as the finest of any British rider until 2012. Millar's exploits in continental Europe helped boost the profile of cycling in Scotland, with his sporting prowess actually making it into mainstream media sports coverage, something that cycling had always struggled to do.

After three seasons as a pro with Peugeot in France, Millar had won a stage of the 1983 Tour de France, his first participation in the race. Anecdotally, there is no doubt that at least one future Glasgow Wheeler was inspired enough by a Scottish television clip on the evening of 11 July 1983 to seek out a local club and start learning the rules of the road. It is impossible to imagine that the author was the only one similarly motivated by Millar's joyous and rather wobbly victory salute in Bagnères-de-Luchon on that warm summer night.

Millar's presence in the Tour de France peloton that year actually owed much to the last Glasgow Wheeler to race as a professional for the French team with its iconic *maillot a damiers,* that draughts/chess board design jersey. When the teenage Millar decided that a career as a professional cyclist was his goal, he made his way to Bilsland.

Back in 1975, the then junior Millar joined the Wheelers, although the Pollokshaws rider's first club was in fact the Glenmarnock

Wheelers, with its clubrooms near Kings Park on Glasgow's south side. John Storrie, that early BLRC road race pioneer, an international road man and indefatigable talent scout, would always claim he had discovered and nurtured Millar's earliest riding days.

Speaking in 2022, York hits a blank. "I don't even know how it happened, I don't even remember the introduction, I just – somehow – ended up on a Glenmarnock club run with John Storrie and you think 'Oh, this is alright. But…I want to go faster. Because I'm only interested in going faster, I wasn't interested in sitting beside a loch with my tin of soup! I was your typical 16-year-old teenager, but I hadn't done any cycling before that. I think I did six races as a junior for the Glenmarnock and then my ambition kicked in," chuckles York, "and I thought, I'd quite like to do this – but do it faster and learn about that, but I can't learn about it from John Storrie with his mudguards because I'm not really a mudguards person (to this day). So the 16-year-old me saw that the Glasgow Wheelers were one of the most dominant clubs and they had Billy Bilsland the ex-pro. So I thought, 'Well, who am I going to learn from?' because I had already decided that I was going to be a professional bike rider. That was it. I had *decided* – that's what I want to do."

In 1976, Millar scored his first mention in the minutes of the club annual general meeting when Billy Bilsland, offering his race secretary's report explained that "we had only one junior member competing, Robert Millar, who had won the Scottish junior road race championship, who had in addition won a few senior road races and had finished second in the junior time trial best all rounder competition."

Well, the Wheelers may only have had one racing junior, but he looked like a good one and, in fact, Millar won both the junior and senior club road race champion titles that season. And the junior time trial championship as well as the fastest '25' recorded by anyone in the club that season – a 58-48. There were no tri-bars, no deep section rims or aero bikes in 1976. You had to feel a little sorry for Ashley McGowan, another talented junior of the era who ran into Millar, though McGowan did win the club hill climb title that year by way of consolation.

York was in no doubt about a career, even from that early age. "I went to school and told my pals that was going to be a professional bike rider. Not that I was going to 'try' to be a pro or that I 'wanted' to be a professional, I just told them that that was what I was *going* to be. Of course they just laughed."

But why quit the Glenmarnock for the Glasgow Wheelers? "That was the big racing club at the time, those were the guys I saw in races riding well and wining, so I figured that they must know what it takes. Plus, I knew that Billy (Bilsland) had been a pro rider, so he must know something. I had no clue who Arthur (Campbell) was when I joined up. I went to Billy and told him and Arthur that I wanted to be a professional and they just kind of nodded." The freshly-minted junior rider wasn't the first one to have announced their ambition to Bilsland, who had heard it all before, yet he was patient and even-handed with the new recruit to the Wheelers racing ranks.

If schoolfriends mocked and Bilsland remained neutral, York set about listening and learning, applying Bilsland's training advice and starting to understand the philosophy and outlook required to make it to the professional ranks. "Both Billy and Arthur explained that I had to move up the different levels as quickly as possible and not hang around. Learn to race, then learn to race in the front, then win the races, move up to the next level and do it again and see how far I could get. So you race in Scotland, win races and then go down South to race. The first year I went down to England I watched these guys ride off up the road, I knew I had to be there, I knew which moves I needed to be in, but I wasn't strong enough. Next year, with another winter's training, I came back stronger and got in the moves and the English guys didn't know who I was. I started getting noticed and winning a couple of races. And then, rather than hang around and race in England, it was time to move to France. Time to move up to the next level and start the process again."

Millar was a prodigious talent and this, allied to a ruthless streak that was essential to making progress, saw him exploit that talent as far as it would go. The ability was clear and the progress linear. At the 1978 Tour of the Trossachs, the classic end of season hilly time trial around Aberfoyle and Calendar, Millar handed a one minute beating to Sandy Gilchrist who had won the previous six editions of the 26 mile race and broke the course record en route to handing a beating to the talented Gilchrist. Millar had just turned 20 and it wrapped up a season in which he had become the first ever Scot to win the British national road race (with Gilchrist in fourth and McGahan in fifth), followed that with a two-minute solo win the brutally tough Tour of the Peak in Derbyshire and a second place in the three-lap Isle of Man international behind the experienced Englishman Steve Lawrence. In between he had finished tenth overall in the Tour of Scotland (which was a pro-am) which made him the best amateur rider in the field. There was a 23rd place in the 1978 Commonwealth Games road race in Edmonton, Canada, a little over a minute behind winner (and future club and pro team mate) Phil Anderson. And, almost as a footnote, he had finished second behind McGahan in the Scottish national road race. Having obtained most of those results as a 19-year-old, it was clear to anyone with eyes to see that Millar had a special talent.

Following the advice of Bilsland and Campbell not to rest on laurels, Millar then made the jump from the UK to France, having clearly taken his British amateur career as far as it could go. Given the calibre of the British races the 19-year-old Millar had won he had seen little point in hanging about. Being a big fish in a small pond was never part of his master plan. Europe – specifically Paris – was calling. In January 1979 he flew to Paris to ride for the fearsome and uncompromising ACBB club, where he shared a basic apartment with ambitious Australian Phil Anderson, like Millar just 20 years old and much further from home.

Recalling life with Peugeot and then Panasonic today, Philippa York explains that Bilsland and Campbell had told him how to negotiate the murky waters of pro cycling politics and etiquette. "It's like a pie chart, you know? You have this massive part of the professional rider pie chart which is basically a jungle where you have to eat or be eaten. Every pro is in there and they all need to have that jungle mentality, but there still needs to be a little slice of that pie chart where you are a decent human being. But, as a pro, if the 'nice' slice of the pie chart was too big, then you didn't do so well in that jungle. When Billy would talk about levels of 'commitment' what he really meant was that you had to be ruthless. Phil Anderson was more ruthless than me but, for example, (Australian fellow pro) Allan Peiper wasn't ruthless enough, that pie chart of his had too big a slice of nice," York laughs.

In fact, for all Millar's high profile heroics in the 1980 and early 1990s, you could argue that the more influential name in terms of his long term impact on Scottish cycling and the Glasgow Wheelers is still that of Bilsland, Millar's mentor and coach. Clearly Millar was a much more successful rider who enjoyed a far longer professional career than Bilsland, but in terms of coaching, support, advice and the flat-out subsidising of riders over decades, Bilsland worked closer to Scottish grass roots racing than Millar.

Any rider who hoped to find a slot on a French team or who needed advice or a frame on long-term loan almost inevitably found himself in Bilsland's shop in the Saltmarket. Bilsland knew what it took to win and survive and when it came to connections, between Bilsland and his father-in-law Arthur Campbell, their network was unsurpassed, not only in Scotland, but in the UK.

For Anglo riders hoping to make the grade in Europe, mental toughness counted for a lot too – you weren't going to go home to your mum after a race when you were a Brit, Irishman, Dane or Australian riding for a European team. Millar was one of many riders Bilsland coached and mentored en route to his 1980 pro contract with Peugeot. "Oh you definitely needed someone who knew what was waiting for the newbie. You still do," insists York today.

Back when it was time for Millar to quit Glasgow and head to France in 1979, he would find a berth at the Parisian ACBB club which by then had turned into the Peugeot team's feeder club of choice. Like Bilsland, Millar had Campbell in his corner, as well as Bilsland and Millar recognises the role that both played in his career.

"Billy played a different role to Arthur, but then the sum of that was I received the guidance needed on what was required. Billy advised on the toughness and training aspects, prepared me for what lay ahead and Arthur added some kind of control and limits to the required harshness that then developed. I know that it might seem strange, as I was a twat at times, but without the political and social awareness that Arthur managed to instil in me, I would have been so much more uncompromising," recalls York. "When I was getting too big for my boots, Arthur would bring me down, keep me balanced and my feet on the ground. Arthur was a great politician, he'd tell me who I needed to keep an eye on. I remember him telling me not to piss off Hein Verbruggen who Arthur had worked out very early on. He told me that Verbruggen was 'just passing through' the UCI on his way to the International Olympic Committee executive. Bearing that in mind he said that I shouldn't upset him, don't do anything to bring yourself to his attention, don't let him know who you are, because he's on his way to the IOC. And I was thinking, 'What are you on about Arthur!?' So Arthur explained it to me that people chose a sport to administer and, at UCI level, it's small money you know? To make things happen sometimes it would take small donations to someone's favourite charity, but at IOC level it's more about 'Would you like a holiday home in Antigua?!' After Arthur had explained that to me, I looked at Verbruggen differently! Mind you, I still upset Verbruggen because, as a young athlete, I was an arsehole at the time, but that's one of the things that comes with the ruthlessness you need. Now, neither Billy nor Arthur would never say that about me, they'd talk about 'the commitment I needed' but what they meant was that I was ruthless enough to climb the ladder. It wasn't a case of ethics or morality, it's just being able to put up with all the other crap or ignore it. I was able to say 'I don't care about what you think or do, I don't care about you taking that bribe to win that race or doing me over for two minutes, I'm looking to the next year, in fact, the next five years. So when Billy and Arthur would tell people I had 'the right attitude' what they meant was that I was an arsehole," laughs York. Almost forty years on, York's attitude has changed, happily for all concerned.

"The thing is, you are always going to upset some people on the way up, but you have to be careful. I didn't leave any of my teams on bad terms with them, I think I could have come back to them (which he did when he returned to ride for 'Z' which, by then, had replaced Peugeot as a sponsor), you needed to be ruthless, but you had to be decent too. I remember thanking Vincent Lavenu, who's now the boss at AG2R, when he rode for me at Fagor and he told me that was the fist time any team leader had ever thanked him in his career." The law of the jungle was – and in pro cycling remains – kill or be killed, but somehow among all the blood, guts and ethical carnage you still had to remember to look after your friends.

Summing up her feelings for Bilsland, York notes that "The respect I have for Billy is immense, in fact he's probably the person that I respect the most in cycling's little world. He's a seriously underrated rider who, if he had been Belgian, would have had a long career, I might have been lucky to have had more basic talent, but Billy was way tougher."

For his part, Bilsland's professional career had come to a conclusion in 1974 after a slow falling out with Raleigh's boss Peter Post. The Dutchman had carved a career as someone capable of driving a hard bargain, whose famously 'tough' persona was in no small part down to him skimming a percentage of his rider's wages and indulging in outrageous favouritism. Post, who was more than happy to cultivate his 'no-nonsense' image, was not a fan of anglophone riders. Disillusioned by Post's wheeler-dealing, though far from finished physically, Bilsland returned to Scotland, living in Dullatur and opening his bike shop in the Saltmarket. Funnily enough, initially it was a Peugeot dealership rather than a Raleigh one.

Bilsland's son Neil – who took over running the Saltmarket shop in 2006 – recalls that "One summer my dad came home and started helping out selling cars for Arthur and made more money in that short period than he did trying to beat Merckx and his men." After doing the hard yards as an amateur and then as a Scotsman in the most French of French cycling teams, Bilsland's head was turned in a car showroom.

"It was actually one winter, in the close season," recalls Bilsland. "Arthur and I had driven into Glasgow to check out a couple of cars and he said, 'OK, you buy that one and drive it back.' So I bought a car for £80 and drove it back to Arthur's coachworks. We tidied it up a bit and priced it at £180. That same day a fella came in, asked for a test, I ended up driving him home, he paid me for the car and then he drove me back to Glasgow! Well, that got me thinking...".

When Bilsland finally returned to Scotland he never raced again, not even at club confined events organised by the Wheelers. Not that he stopped riding and training with the top tier at the club. Though, in the end, even that had its limits, as Bilsland recalls. "I remember one winter we were going round the coast (down the A77, down to Largs and back through Greenock to Glasgow). A few of the guys turned back at Kilmarnock, but Robert (Millar), Jamie McGahan, Colin Fraser and myself kept going. Well, there were sparks coming off Jamie that day, so when I got back to Cumbernauld I thought I should do a bit more. And as I was riding the extra miles I just thought to myself, 'Is it not time to stop this?!' It wasn't that the roads were icy, but it was minus 10 or something – and that was it for me."

Initially he worked alongside his father-in-law, in Arthur's car dealership on Duke Street, before he opened up the Saltmarket bike shop in 1979. "It was actually Sammy McLatchie who put the idea in my head. Sammy had been a real strong rider, but he had a shoe shop in Kirkintilloch and also had an account with some bike firms. Anyway, he said opening a bike shop would be worth a go. So when they revamped the shops at the Saltmarket, I took one on." Bilsland, with no retail experience, tempted Rattray's fixture and fellow Wheeler Jackie Potter to help out and, as if by magic, Bilsland found himself with a new customer base.

As well as selling a stack of Peugeots, Bilsland quietly began helping riders behind the scenes as well as organising and sponsoring the races. None of the new breed of hopefuls quite turned out to be of the same calibre as Millar, but there weren't many west of Scotland riders who didn't end up in Bilsland's shop, asking for advice or components on generous zero-percent credit terms that was never means tested.

In a cardboard box, tucked away somewhere, there's his famous Black Book. This was the dog-eared, hardback A4 diary containing the names of the great, the good and the decidedly average, listed beside monies owed for Vittoria Corsa CX tubulars and Campag Super Record chainsets, paid off a few quid at a time, whenever Department of Health and Social Security cheques, student grant or prize money allowed. There were no credit checks or forms signed and initialled of course, just a remarkable level of trust.

There were plenty of riders who earned a few quid under the counter to supplement the State's meagre 'Supplementary benefit' by helping out at the Saltmarket shop too. There were several riders from the west of Scotland for whom Bilsland gave as much help as he could – a bit of cash-in-hand work, discount components, tubulars and frames as well as training advice. If riders didn't quite make it like Bilsland or Robert Millar did, it wasn't because Bilsland didn't do what he could for them.

There's an argument to be made that, throughout the 1980s, thousands of British cyclists – including many internationals and elite riders – were effectively 'State-sponsored' albeit unofficially and on only £22 a week! The DHSS Wheelers, the largest club membership in Britain, all categories welcome.

At the same time as Millar had been finding his feet, he was joined at the Wheelers by fellow Glaswegian Jamie McGahan. It turns out that McGahan had been going out for rides with an elderly neighbour who was a dyed-in-the-wool cycle tourer. One day in 1975 the pair were twiddling along and were caught by Pat McCabe on the Garscube road, a Wheelers mainstay since the 1923 season and a man who had won more than his fair share of races, including Scottish track championships. McCabe was, simply, a racing legend from the 1930s, one of those BLRC pioneers. Of all the riders for McGahan to borrow a frame pump from...

McGahan recalls his baptism, his conversion from riding an old Flying Scot to a stripped down racing bike. One day he was a tourist but, after meeting McCabe, racing consumed him. He was 15-years-old. "I was living in a tenement in Possil and had noticed this old guy in plus fours riding an immaculate bike, going out in the mornings and coming back at night. I'd ask him where he had been and he would tell me he had been to Endrick water or wherever and that was it – I wanted to be a cyclist. So my dad bought me one of the neighbour's old frames – a 23 and a half inch frame that was about two inches too big for me, but that was it."

The young McGahan had no immediate urge to be a racing cyclist, rather he was happy to ride his bike and be part of cycling club culture. "The plan? The plan was just to be a cyclist. I would go down to the club nights at Springburn Sports centre and be mesmerised by all the bikes there – the Flying Scots and Hetchins."

The social side of those club nights, the regular presence of Bilsland and Campbell as well as tales told over tea and coffee all appealed to the young McGahan. "It wasn't a big racing club at the time," recalls McGahan, "not at the time. Billy had just finished his professional career and there were a few guys racing, doing 12 Hours and all sorts, but I wouldn't say there were any big hitters at the club when I joined."

As has been noted elsewhere, cycling clubs were not exclusively about road racing and time trialling. The weekend club runs and hostelling weekends were undertaken by riders who would happily race on other weekends. This was Scottish cycling club culture of the era. As McGahan reveals.

"A week after I joined the club, a few weeks after my sixteenth birthday, some of the guys were riding to Oban. I had got a few bob for my birthday, so off I went with them. I got the knock and punctured and by the time I got to Crianlarich I had spent most of my money – but they had waited on me." In the mid-1970s the trial by torture of new recruits was still in vogue. You hung on till you got dropped, you rode on and hoped that at some point you would find your new clubmates at a shop or cafe. You *hoped*. As it turned out, not many of his new club mates would be dropping young McGahan for much longer. Barely a year after McGahan joined the Wheelers he had won his first prize, on that same oversized Flying Scot frame.

"I remember it so well," laughs McGahan, retired from a teaching career and living in Dunoon. "I won the handicap in a '10' with a 26-18 down in Ayr and won an Oppy cap and some chamois cream with a foreign name. I thought I was big time!"

Inside the club there was encouragement of racing and McGahan had showed enough promise for de facto club coach Jimmy Dorward to start to offer advice and Dorward took McGahan and another rider, Colin Fraser, down to the British junior road race championship in 1976. It was the start of a fruitful if fractious relationship with Dorward.

"Jimmy had me doing weights in his garage and then tea and scones after the session," explains McGahan, "it was a little bit of luxury for me and Jimmy was generous with his time." But he was a hard task master too. "Jimmy was really keen on interval training, that was a big part of his training. Three minute efforts around the graveyard (the infamous 'triangle' around Cadder cemetery near Bishopbriggs) and I always give it everything. Mind you, I remember thinking once, 'This never stops, where was it leading?' you know. I was doing intervals all year, from before the start of the season all the way through it. It never stopped!"

Between Dorward's relentless training regime and McGahan's natural talent, the 17-year-old junior Wheeler from Possil would end up winning senior races and making a name for himself.

"The week before the senior road race championship in 1977 I was 18 and got disqualified from second place behind (future Scottish national road manager) Ian Thomson. "He had beaten me in a two-up sprint, Ian was a big strong guy and I said 'Bastard!' as I crossed the line. I got disqualified and someone took the mickey out of me when I said I wanted to make a written appeal. I was out of order, but there you go, these things happen in the heat of the moment. Anyway, I was dejected and feeling like the world was against me, but the next weekend I beat Robert Millar in the sprint for the national road race title up in Dundee. The previous weekend I had been disqualified and ridiculed and then seven days later I went home with a national champions jersey at 18. It was a magical moment!"

McGahan was nearing the end of his short spell with the Wheelers, but then so was his coach, Dorward. A man of strong will and innovative ideas, the Bishopbriggs-based Dorward left the Wheelers to form the Scotia CC and, in due course, McGahan followed him. It did not end well.

"I was selected to ride the Tour of Britain for Scotland in 1978 and Jimmy was to be the team manager. I didn't have a clue how to hold my place in the bunch against all those Russians, Poles and Czechs and we were getting a hard time, getting dropped early on. I was doing OK, finishing in the bunch, but Jimmy accused me of not trying. We were at the digs one day and he said, 'If you were trying you'd be falling in your soup right now.' I was shocked, because I was trying all right. I was always able to recover well every day and getting round, but I felt so bad I remember actually just letting go on a stage, faking that I was done in, just to 'prove' I was trying hard. And they took the piss out of me for 'getting dropped.' It was terrible."

Things went from bad to worse for the Scotland team. Young Bobby Melrose abandoned, and two Edinburgh riders Maurice Laing and Rab McLeod were sent home by Dorward after they went out to a disco on the rest day and missed Dorward's clear 10pm curfew. By the time the race finished in Blackpool only McGahan and Robert Millar had lasted the distance. The pair of 19-year-old Glasgow Wheelers finished 54th and 19th respectively, in a race won by Polish man-mountain Jan Brzezny. "I thought my career was over," recalls McGahan. How wrong he was, albeit for his many future successes he wouldn't be wearing a Wheelers jersey.

Still advised by Bilsland and Campbell, McGahan tried his luck down on the cote d'Azur, with a club based in Nice, a club berth which Campbell, inevitably, had helped find. In February 1979, the club's monthly minutes note "W. Bilsland reports that Robert Millar and Jamie McGahan had gone to France to further their cycling careers. A collection had been taken during the club night prior to J. McGahan's departure and £32.50 was given to J. McGahan to help him with his travelling expenses."

Sadly, McGahan never found his feet in France nor, later, after trying his luck on the cobbles of Belgium in the company of Fraser.

Millar and McGahan aside, at the domestic level, the Wheelers continued to do well, in terms of member numbers, though there were clouds on the horizon for the Wheelers as well as every other club. Between 1950 and 1970 car ownership in the UK had tripled and, since 1985, the number of cars on Scottish roads has doubled, from 1.5 million, to three million. For context, there are now (2021) around 30 million cars and vans on Britain's roads. When today's parents fret about letting their offspring ride on roads because they seem so busy, they have a point. Within the cycling career of most adults, traffic volumes on Scottish roads have doubled. We're still riding on the same road to Aberfoyle, but there are now twice as many cars trying to overtake us.

On a personal note, in as much as it had little direct impact on the club, in 1976 Campbell was awarded an MBE for services to cycling. Perhaps more significant – and more useful in terms of networking – in 1977 Campbell was elected to the post of Chairman of the UCI Technical committee, having been a member of it for several years. It meant a lot of travelling and it wasn't always travelling that Campbell wanted to do.

Thus, if there was a new velodrome in Caracas that needed to be checked over, Campbell might pass the trip to a comrade in Czechoslovakia. It always paid to make friends, because friends and influence meant invitations for Scottish teams and riders.

Not that Campbell's politicking always paid off and on one occasion his efforts to help a friend from the Eastern Bloc ended up with a visit from Special Branch. Campbell had put a Soviet UCI delegate in touch with a computer firm because the Russian wanted to buy an up-to-date computer and take it back to the USSR. It was purchased and all above board, the Russian paid for the new computer and had receipts, but he never got past customs at Heathrow and, back in Kirkintilloch, Campbell got a knock on his door asking about a Russian they had in custody who claimed to know him…

With the departure of Millar and McGahan, all was not lost on the racing front. The presence of Bilsland and Campbell inside the club – allied to the professional exploits of Millar on continental Europe – meant that the Wheelers still had pull. It was still a jersey that people wanted to ride in.

And, for a brief couple of seasons in the late 1978s, it was a jersey that was adorned with the name 'OC Plastics' a west of |Scotland business. Inevitably, the sponsorship arrived via Campbell. It turns out that Mr OC Plastics was Tommy O'Connell, a friend of Jackie Connor, a long-time sponsor of the Regent CC and, having shown an interest in sponsorship of a local club, Jackie mentioned this to Arthur and, before you could say 'Just sign here and initial there' the Glasgow Wheelers had a sponsor. O'Connell had been living abroad for a few years but, on his return to the old country in early 1977, he signed up and handed over a cheque for £500.

The year that Millar's name first turns up in the membership book, he was one of new fewer than 21 young riders. Yes, *twenty-one* junior and schoolboy riders. Clearly, not all of them were destined for Continental careers, but many were – and remained – keen club riders. One such was Tom Scott, from Springburn, whose career as a cyclist was sparked in 1974 when he first joined the club as a 15-year-old schoolboy, following in the slipstream of his school pal Robert Thayne.

"Sunday morning club runs for younger riders started from Stirling library in Royal Exchange square and they were always organised by Pat McCabe, who'd turn up on his classic orange Jack Taylor bike," recalls Scott. "Other times we'd all go away hostelling with Mick McLaughlin as well."

McCabe, who had first joined the Wheelers in 1923, had performed just about every role in the club, from president to chairman and just about everything in between. Under McCabe's guidance riders would head out north to Fintry or Flanders Moss, Aberfoyle, west to Kilmacolm, south down to Fenwick or up north to Glen Fruin, Inverbeg or a longer ride to Killearn. And, at every destination, McCabe knew the drum-up spot. "We would all be sent to look for wood for the drum by Pat who built the fire. We'd make toast by sticking a twig through the bread and holding it to the fire. Tea was in a Billy can, but that had to be christened when it was new. You can being 'christened' meant it was kicked about till it was 'broken in'!"

When it came to 'breaking in' it wasn't just the Billy cans that got the treatment, albeit riders were also 'broken in' in a very different fashion. It was riders like McCabe – and there were men like Pat in most clubs of the era – who would show youngsters how to ride in a bunch. There was a lot to learn about cadence, about gear choice, tyres, tyre pressures, how to corner, how to ride through-and-off, wheeling about in a crosswind, how not to 'drop' your bike when you got out of the saddle, how to set your bike and brakes up, how to glue tubular tyres and…the list was almost endless. But the wealth of knowledge, tips and tricks gathered by McCabe and his peers over decades of riding was inculcated into newcomers in the course of those long club rides and drum-ups.

And then there was the racing. "There were club-confined handicap races – APRs – on Wednesday nights where we'd race in groups, though they weren't that long," continues Scott. "We'd start in Torrance and race round the Campsie glen. I remember Robert Millar rode one night and he was in the 'scratch' group – just him. He told me later he only used the wee ring! We did club confined 10 mile time trials too, starting at Torrance roundabout, straight out – John Thayne was always the timekeeper, like he was in the APRs."

Having just called time on his professional career, Billy Bilsland was back and helping out the club by 1975. "Billy would take us to schoolboy races in a mini bus. We went to Glenrothes, Bellahouston park and Springburn park. He'd fix our gears before we went – we were limited to 78-inch maximum (that's a 52x18) and there was always a gear check beforehand. Billy would sort our gears in his kitchen in Dullatur. He gave John Duncan, another junior, a set of wheels and a Peugeot frame. Mind you, I was lucky enough to be the same shoe size as Billy, so he gave me his cycling shoes, which was lucky, since I was racing in Hush Puppy trainers at the time."

Around the age of 17, Scott got into skateboarding and, being better on four wheels and trucks than two wheels and tubs, Scott ended up as a sponsored boarder and travelled around the UK competing. "My cycling claim to fame was coming second as a 15-year-old junior in the Scottish roller championships at the John Wright sports centre in East Kilbride, behind Ed Hood (later of the *Velo Veritas* website), but I didn't like hurting myself in training and was therefore never destined to be any good!"

While none of those junior racing members would scale the dizzy (Pyrenean) heights of Millar, future Scottish champions rode in the iconic jersey described in the SCU handbook as 'a royal blue band and piping on a white jersey.' Schoolboy John Duncan – the happy recipient of Bilsland's Peugeot – was certainly the most promising of the new wave. In 1977 he won the national Schoolboy '10' time trial and the TT BAR title too. Moving up an age category, Duncan finished third in the Scottish junior road race in 1979 and, for good measure, won the junior Best All-Rounder road race series. It wasn't that much of a shock, since Duncan had won the club hill-climb as a schoolboy the previous season and backed up Robert Millar as the second counter in the Wheelers team who carried off the Scottish national hill-climb in 1977 (which Millar won). Duncan was destined to be a character whose star blazed brightly but briefly, as that schoolboy and junior rider promise failed to make the transition to senior racing. In large part down to going off to Aberdeen university and being pre-ordained to work on the family dairy farm. "I remember one day we had ridden up to Arrochar," recalls his then mentor Billy Bilsland, "and he turned to me and asked if we'd be back in time for him to help with the evening milking. At that point you sort of realised where his priorities were going to be, whether he wanted it or not."

However, at the dawn of the 1980s, in fact in precisely 1980, three other schoolboy riders from the club were SCU time trial BAR team champions. Mike Lawson, Iain Thayne (son of John and Johan) and Alan Fairweather (son of Alfie) came out on top. The young trio were awarded their prize at the end of that season by Alan Wells, the 1980 Olympic sprint champion, the Scot who had taken on the Soviets and beaten them at their own Games, in every sense.

Of the trio, it was Lawson who would go on to have more success, both as a junior and as a senior international. In fact, though nobody could know at the time, it was Wheelers of that generation – Lawson and Neil MacLeod – who would be the last to claim medals at the Scottish national senior road race championship – and Lawson was the last to take the title. As the 1980s came to a close, the Wheelers road racing presence, internationally and domestically, began to recede. Well, we'd had a good run.

7

TO THE CENTRE OF THE CITY

IF THE WHEELERS successes both domestically and internationally began to diminish in the later 1980s, cycling as a sport was doing rather well. As had often been the case with cycling – and other sports – it was about to undergo a surge in popularity. From time to time, for reasons that are scarcely fathomable and far less predictable, a sport undergoes a growth spurt. From BMX to skateboarding via basketball and American football, for a period of time a minority sport will burst into UK cultural consciousness, achieving stratospheric growth and wide media coverage. Some stay the course, others return to oblivion or faddish cult status, lying dormant until they are reawakened, propelled back into the spotlight by an ambitious marketing team and a pot of new sponsorship money. Cycling has never been immune from these unpredictable surges.

In the middle 1980s cycling's moment in the sun came thanks in no small part to a former Glasgow Wheeler, with a little help from the arrival of a free-to-air UK television channel launched in 1982. The twin impacts of Robert Millar's European exploits and Channel Four's regular cycling coverage were to give Scottish – and British – cycling a healthy boost.

It's only in retrospect that we can see how significant the years between 1983 and 1985 were in boosting the popularity of road cycling. In those seasons, the career of Millar, the launch of new magazines ('*Cyclist*', '*Bicycle Action*' and '*Winning*' to name three) as well as Chanel Four's decision to broadcast Tour de France highlights and its own city centre criterium series put road racing squarely in the public eye. When you add that decades' strong continental anglophone contingent including Sean Kelly, Phil Anderson, Greg Lemond, Allan Peiper, Paul Sherwen, Sean Yates, Graham Jones, John Herety, Martin Earley and Stephen Roche, the popularity of the sport could hardly fail to be raised.

Additionally, Channel Four's Kellogg's city centre criterium series was populated by a domestic professional class of between 40 and 50 riders, who also enjoyed a healthy British professional race calendar. Given those factors, its no surprise that the membership of Scottish cycling clubs experienced an increase.

The impact of increased media coverage stimulated by anglophone stars performing at the highest level cannot be underestimated. In a similar way, a still more impressive hike in the profile and popularity of cycling would occur in 2012 with the London Olympics and Bradley Wiggins' and Team Sky's stellar season. By then however British Cycling was funded to the tune of tens of millions of pounds of government-channelled National Lottery cash.

However, back in the early 1980s Glasgow Wheelers stalwarts Peter Harley and Alfie Fairweather were still performing creditably in time trials in all distances. Fairweather, who had been racing and winning in Wheelers colours since 1960 as a junior, set the men's Scottish '50' mile time trial in 1978 with 1-56-13, a mark that lasted for eight years until Davie Millar of the Chryston Wheelers improved it by 15 seconds. Fairweather was still a formidable performer in time trials and road races, setting a 100 mile Scottish time trial record in 1981 at the age of 41 with a 4-15-00. Scottish road surfaces, wind and weather were rarely conducive to records but Fairweather (and Harley) were tenacious and talented. You don't set medium- and long-distance time trial records because you got lucky with heavier than usual dual-carriageway traffic on a 'float' day...

Throughout the early to mid-1980s the Wheelers had an active membership that fluctuated at around 60, with a mix of youth and experience that is unlikely to be seen again (for demographic reasons if nothing else).

Millar's performances in the Tours of the 1980s had raised both his and cycling's profile and it shone a little light on the Wheelers too. His appearance at the Kellogg's City Centre criterium around George Square – which included the 'climb' of North Frederick street in 1984 – saw crowds three deep around the circuit. That same summer Channel 4 had televised a 30-minute highlights package of the Tour de France, introducing cycling to a new audience and moving it slightly closer to the UK sporting mainstream. If there were new and curious riders joining cycling clubs in those years, there were still others who had entered the sport by more traditional means – principally because family members were already involved.

To pluck four young names almost at random from this era, we could cite Iain Thayne (of the clan Thayne) Alan Fairweather (son of Alfie), Martin Coll (whose dad Joe had joined the Wheelers in 1952) and Mike Lawson, whose father and older brother had introduced him to the sport. Coll junior was never a Wheeler, though the others wore the colours with distinction.

Lawson would be a future Scottish road champion and Commonwealth Games rider, paying his club dues as a schoolboy (what in 2023, would be a 'youth' licence) rider in 1979. In fact Lawson was part of the Glasgow Wheelers winning Schoolboy Best-All Rounder time trial team of 1980. The other young Wheelers being Iain Thayne and Alan Fairweather.

By then the Lawson family was based in Cumbernauld, but Mike's older brother Stewart and dad Frank had been members of the Fullarton Wheelers and raced for the Ayrshire club. Although the youngest Lawson joined the Wheelers in 1979 as a schoolboy, he had actually met Bilsland and Arthur Campbell several years earlier, on Mallorca.

"I think I was about eight or nine at the time and we were on holiday in Magaluf in February 1974. I spotted some men dropping off their key at reception as they tottered on cycling shoes. So I went up to them and said with the naivety of a yokel, "Are you cyclists, because my brother's a cyclist too". The fit-looking man asked what club my brother was in and what his name was. I said, 'Stewart Lawson and he's in the Fullarton Wheelers. What club are you in, mister?' He replied 'My name's Billy and I'm in the Glasgow Wheelers.' He told me his name was Billy Bilsland, though I heard it as *Bisland*. When I told my parents, my old man says 'Billy Bilsland, the pro?' It turns out Billy was over in Magaluf with Arthur Campbell, Jackie Connor and Sammy McLatchie. For the rest of the stay, the deal was that I would clean their bikes after each ride and they gave me a few pesetas. So that was my introduction to Billy and Arthur."

A few months later the Lawson family moved from Ayrshire to Dullatur, coincidentally – and, as it turned out, conveniently – close to Bilsland. In due course Stewart Lawson, then racing as a junior, packed up and the cycling baton in the Lawson household was picked up by Mike.

In the tight-knit world of Scottish cycling of the era, it seemed like everyone knew everyone else who rode. At school Lawson discovered he was sitting beside the daughter of Frank Lafferty, Lorraine, whose dad was the sponsor of the Glenmarnock CC on Glasgow's south side, the first cycling club that Robert Millar had raced for. Small world indeed.

Young Lawson, still not quite 11, started riding with another north Lanarkshire local, John Duncan. Duncan was three years older than Lawson, but they explored the roads around Cumbernauld and beyond. Lawson recalls one ride with Bilsland and Arthur Campbell "They went round Alloa and Larbert and back and kept looking back to see if I was still there." Although by that point the Scotia was already well-established having been formed by Jimmy Dorward – Lawson and Duncan joined the Wheelers.

"Billy would chat with John (Duncan) and me and he finally offered to get us into a club so that we wouldn't just be going for rides on our own. He said we could go with him to the Glasgow Wheelers or go to another club called the Scotia at Bishopbriggs where his old coach Jimmy Dorward was. Billy even took me in to a club night in the Bishopbriggs sports centre to see the Scotia. John didn't see any reason to go elsewhere other than the Wheelers with Billy and that's what we did. So probably from the winter of 1975-1976, Billy would take John and me into the Wheeler's club nights. He would stop off in Kirkintilloch to pick up Arthur on the way. Monday nights in the Springburn Sports Centre. I remember the names and some of the faces of the adult stalwart members of the club – Jimmy Brinkins, Pat McCabe, Joe McCann, Ashby McGowan, the Thayne family and Tommy Banks." It's remarkable that 40 years later those names were – and are still – part of the Wheelers.

Like Jamie McGahan, Lawson recalls the club nights and cycling club culture with some fondness and clarity – in the 1970s and 1980s a cycling club was more than just a jersey you wore and annual subs you paid. "At that time, Billy (Bilsland) seemed to be interested in developing the young riders in the club and he used to organise weight training sessions at the club night to initiate the kids. The bar would be set up and the youngsters would line up and do the exercises in turn, military curls, press-behind-the-neck, bent-back rowing. Afterwards it was tea and biscuits in the clubroom."

But of course for most Glasgow Wheelers, the weekend club run was the centre of interest – not everyone was racing and not everyone was racing every weekend. "There were Sunday club runs that John (Duncan) and I did with a fair amount of youngsters. I seem to remember it was Pat McCabe who officiated. There were drum-ups at the Lake of Mentieth, on the Carron Valley at a wee burn just after the bridge after Fintry at the start of the Carron Valley road, at Balmaha too. I remember Billy pushed me up the 1-in-8 climb at Balmaha while sitting in the saddle!"

Also like McGahan, Lawson would eventually join the Scotia and be coached by Dorward and, like McGahan before him, his relationship with the coach would be beneficial, but fraught. In fact, throughout the 1980s Dorward gave enormous amounts of time and energy to cycling, whether at the Wheelers or his own club, the Scotia. There's a strong argument that Dorward was the most important and influential Scottish cycling coach of the post-war era.

Andy Ferry, who only ever rode with the Scotia and was trained, like Lawson, by Dorward observes that "it didn't matter to Jimmy what sort of rider you were, he didn't cherry pick looking for another Robert Millar, if you came to the club and showed enthusiasm and commitment, then he would give you all the help you needed. But if you didn't have the level of commitment needed to work with Jimmy then you might as well not bother."

Scottish international David Whitehall – whose son Andrew would ride for the Wheelers some 40 years later – joined the Scotia as a 17-year-old and was another of 'Jimmy's boys.' Whitehall has similar recollections to Ferry. "He would work with anyone who showed commitment, but if he thought you were slacking, it was over. Going round the Cadder graveyard with him on the stopwatch, he'd say that someone was a 'two minute egg' and should just go home. Two minutes was too slow. There were times when I would be 10 or 15 seconds slower than the previous week and he'd just tell us to go home. The fact that I had maybe raced on both Saturday and Sunday and we were back doing intervals on the Tuesday night didn't make a difference. Looking back, we were over-trained I suppose, but at the time nobody knew about that."

Dorward's training sessions on Saturdays were often track-based, at Grangemouth, sessions which would regularly see between 20 and 30 riders attend in the early 1980s. Ferry takes up the story again. "Jimmy did everything. There would be specific training sessions in the morning, then a break for lunch and then, in the afternoon, we'd do races – scratch, handicaps and devils, stuff like that. And Jimmy had it all, all he needed – a stopwatch, a clipboard and a whistle. And after we'd all raced flat out, we'd ride back to Kirkintilloch or Glasgow, wherever."

When Ferry mentions that Dorward "did everything" that would also include throwing salt around the bottom of the track to melt the frost on particularly cold starts on January mornings.

Dorward was always looking for the latest developments in coaching and, in 1982 his riders were confronted with his early heart rate monitor. "Jimmy would flag guys down after an effort on the track and clip a wee gizmo on your ear lobe. You were puffing and panting, propped up against the barrier while it recorded your pulse. Jimmy noted it over a couple of minutes and then off you went again. He never told us the numbers though!" That was a few years before reports of Dr Francesco Conconi's infamous lactate testing and deflection point emerged from Italy and, if Dorward's technique and technology lacked the sophistication of the Italian sports doctor, well, unlike state-funded Conconi, Jimmy was never financed by the British government or British Olympic Association...

Lawson won the Scottish junior road race title in 1982, adding that to junior road race Best All-Rounder championship for the Wheelers. In fact, Lawson, coached by Dorward, won the first six junior or junior/veteran road races of the season, untouchable till May of 1982 (at which point future British Olympian Eddie Alexander did him by half a wheel on a flat course in Edinburgh). Lawson left to join the Scotia and would go on to win the senior road title in 1985 – outsprinting fellow Scotia rider Andy Ferry. There was also a disappointing ride in the 1986 Commonwealth Games road race on a miserable day on the sodden Edinburgh by-pass which today Lawson describes as the low point of his cycling career.

Subsequently Lawson's university studies would take him to Spain (simultaneously racing in Catalunya) finishing off his studies in France, where he married, raised a family, carving a career teaching English in a Metz secondary school.

Although he abandoned cycling for running for several years, his son, Theotime, showed considerable promised as a national-level triathlete, tempting Lawson back on the bike riding with Metz club Velo Sport Montigny.

Lawson had long left the club when, in the mid-1980s, club sponsorship was becoming increasingly common. The Scottish Cyclists' Union, with an eye on boosting its stretched revenues, decided that sponsorship would be OK so long as each club paid a £90 fee to register someone as a sponsor.

For all that the Wheelers jersey had remained unchanged for decades – the classic royal blue chest band and piping on a white jersey – when the Trustee Savings Bank (TSB) came on board in February 1987 the jersey underwent its first significant change. After a meeting at the Trust House Forte hotel (where, inevitably, Arthur Campbell was present) it was agreed that the club would now be known and registered with the SCU as Glasgow Wheelers – Team TSB. Of course there had been a brief period in the late 1970s when the Wheelers had been sponsored, by OC Plastics or O'Connor plastics to give them full credit, but that jersey was still, basically, the classic design. With the arrival of TSB, that was about to change.

Some purists were less than delighted with the style of the new jersey (which had been inspired by the successful British ANC-Halfords pro team design), but it was a sign of the times, and resistance was futile. The minutes of the February 1987 meeting explained that, "TSB was obviously of the opinion that the traditional jersey was not sufficiently eye-catching." TSB's man Neil Boddy, being the piper who was calling the tune, suggested that the blue colour on the new kit would be Pantone 285, the same blue as the TSB logo. The formidable Joe Patterson, a former secretary and treasurer who had been with the Wheelers since 1946, "asked that his dislike of the new jersey should be recorded." And it duly was. And has been again.

In any case, you could still ride and train in the classic top, even if you couldn't *officially* race in it. Which is to say that if you turned up to a race with the 'wrong' jersey, an old design, then the commissaire could refuse you a start. If, on the other hand, the commissaire turned a blind eye, well, carry on.

The TSB was actually a UK-wide banking group, although it had more of a presence in Glasgow, Edinburgh and Belfast than it did in the rest of the UK. As a marketing ploy it made some kind of sense. The initial sum agreed for that first season was £3,000 with £1,500 for the subsequent years of the contract in 1988 and 1989. Doing the decent thing, the club transferred its account from the Bank of Scotland to its new benefactors…

Issues of sponsorship and the distinction between amateur and professionalism had long plagued sport and, with the growth in interest and power of the International Olympic Committee in the mid-1980s (after the revenue-bonanza of the 1984 Los Angeles Games), the terrain was shifting. The line between what constituted a professional and an amateur was blurry and, by 1996 the UCI abolished the distinction completely. From then on, riders were either youth, junior, under-23 or Elite, regardless of your income or sponsorship circumstances.

Although its fair to say that Arthur Campbell wasn't deeply involved in the club's weekly activities in the 1980s, there weren't may clubs who could somehow conjure up Eddy Merckx (1987) as a guest of honour at their annual awards night and club dinner then follow that up the next autumn with Gino Bartali accompanied by the president of the Italian Cycling Federation, Agostino Omini. This was peak Campbell.

It's not hard not see the hand of Campbell in both these appearances and he fended off a gate-crashing *Cycling Weekly* reporter with a stern admonition that Eddy was 'off limits' to questions and that this was strictly a social affair. The author did not dare transgress, while the appearance of Bartali was treated as the Second Coming by the older Wheelers, riders who had been in their prime at the same time as Bartali, star-struck at the ageing Italian's appearance, walking among them in a Glasgow hotel, spirited there by Campbell.

"He was like the king," recalled Brian Smith, a Johnstone Wheeler, of course, but a rider who crossed paths often enough with the globe-trotting Campbell in his UCI Commissaire role. "When Arthur came into a room, he had something about him, and he had all these stories. If you were sitting at a table with Arthur, he was the one holding court. It was always 'Eddy' and never 'Merckx' or it would be 'Bernard' rather than 'Hinault.' It took me a while to work out who he was talking about, it was always first names," laughs Smith.

If Merckx and Bartali were illustrious names from the past, then cycling clubs, built on years of tradition, were about to face significant challenges. The growth in mountain biking, increased traffic volumes and a patchy relationship with her majesty's constabulary meant race organisers were faced with challenging new realities. It was inevitable that as traffic increased on Scottish roads that race organisers were faced with tough choices about the long-established race circuits combined with receding support from local police.

Yet the Wheelers, like so many other cycling clubs, stuck to both guns and traditions. The club weekend club rides and midweek club-confined events that were so many new, young riders first introduction to competition continued. Thus, the 10-year-old Chris Thomson's introduction to racing was at the Wheeler's club long-established Cuilt brae hill climb championship in Lennoxtown. "I didn't even have a bike, but my dad (Hector) and I were there. Anyway, Billy Inches rode the climb, then came back down the hill, passed his bike to me so I could have a go! That was my first ever race! Jamie McGahan won." There was nobody at the Wheelers with any coaching qualifications, nobody was over-concerned about traffic or the absence of child protection officers at the Wheelers (or any other cycling club), for better, for worse, in that era, all you needed to do was turn up and ride.

David Hassan was the Wheelers star in the mid-1980s, being part of the Scottish national quartet which won the British 100km team trial title in 1988 – a rare success for Scottish teams and riders against top-flight English opposition.

Hassan had tried his luck in France with the UC Champenoise near Rheims in 1985, aided, inevitably, by Campbell and Bilsland. Sadly, like McGahan, he never settled, finding neither his feet or the results required to pursue his professional ambitions. It wasn't as if Hassan wasn't talented or lacking form – the day before he left for France the 22-year-old had won the the mid-March 85 mile Best All-Rounder (BAR) road race along the Carron valley and over the Crow Road which had assembled the best roadmen in Scotland at the time. Alas, where both Bilsland and Millar had survived life in the France, Hassan cracked.

Tangentially, Brian Smith, one of Scotland most successful professionals, also got a little help from a Glasgow Wheeler at the dawn of his career. "I think I was about 12 or 13 when I met Pippa – Robert then of course – when he came back from France one winter. Every winter he came back he would be out with the Renfrew bunch and he ended up giving me some kit. In 1987 for some reason a Scottish team got an entry in the Grand Prix d'Isbergues in north east France, racing with Peugeot, Panasonic, Système U, Lotto and the rest. Anyway, Robert came up to me at the start and told me to come and meet Claude Escalon, who was the directeur sportif at the ACBB club in Paris. I had no idea, but Robert had got me a place in the team for the next year."

Back on the domestic scene, veteran Alfie Fairweather and his son Alan were both still active in time trialling and road racing, while Peter Harley was still terrifying juniors with his 'massive' 54-tooth chain ring in time trials. Harley had a golden season in 1982, setting a vet's record at 10 miles with a 21-29, a record that stood for eight years. He also et a '25' vets record that summer too, with a 56-19 in the era with no tri-bars, disc wheels, aero helmets or crazy long socks.

Mike Lawson was winning titles in time trials and road races, a couple of seasons later young junior Gordon Barr (who had joined in 1984) was showing promise on the roads.

13-year-old Bearsden resident Barr had pumped up the tyres on his dad's old touring bike with schoolboy neighbour Michael Bennett and started foraging north towards Loch Lomond. Having dallied with both the Lomond Roads and the Glasgow Nightingale, both youngsters ended up on the Wheelers books in 1984. "The John and Johan Thayne lived close and they got their son Iain to show us the ropes," recalls Barr, "we ended up going round the graveyard to learn how to corner and pedalling cadences. I don't recall many club runs, to be honest, we still went out with the Lomond Roads."

Barr had never been a team sports guy – "I didn't like football" – but had done a bit of running and quickly showed some talent on two wheels."I started doing time trials and was fastest in a few I entered, which got me really keen, and I did a few schoolboy crits around Kings Park and Bellahouston."

Inevitably, Barr was coached by Jimmy Dorward and, as he reached the junior ranks, the benefits of those efforts around the graveyard triangle measured by Dorward's stopwatch paid off. In 1987 Scottish junior road race run around 65 hilly miles on the Cathkin Braes circuit, Dorward gave Barr quite explicit instructions. "It was my first ever road race on open roads and Jimmy told me to attack the first time up the hill. So I did and a couple of other guys came with me. It was a stinking hot day and eventually one of the guys said he was going back to the bunch and the other guy got dropped. I just kept going. Every lap Jimmy would jump out from some bushes and throw cold water at me. My dad was at the top of the hill in a deck chair, but he'd get up to give me two thumbs up every lap. I was away for 64 of the 65 miles, but I held on to win by about two minutes."

Winning your first road race – which just happened to be a national championship – is a decent start to your junior race career. "Actually I felt like a bit of an imposter. I had just attacked and they never caught me, I don't know, it didn't feel right. I was out with Davie Hassan a wee while later and I told him that was how I felt and Davie put me straight!" laughs Barr. "He said, 'You won! You won the race! It doesn't matter *how* you won it. You attacked, they didn't catch you so you won, that's all that matters.' He couldn't understand why I was bothered!"

From that point on Barr enjoyed more than his share of success. In 1986 he had already been club champion in both road race and time trials and when Barr added the 1987 Scottish Best All-Rounder road race championship to his road title, Scottish team selection followed.

By this point, in the late 1980s, the club had attracted a healthy nucleus of young riders with Barr, Stevie Russell and Hawick's Bruce Scott, all of whom would feature in Scottish junior teams of the period. "I'm proud to say that I won an international race in a Scotland jersey," notes Barr, "a stage in the Hoffman's International over in Ireland!"

There were racing trips down to England too, competing in the Peter Buckley series and later, as a senior, a victory in the 1990 edition of the Drummond Trophy as well as medals in the national cyclo-cross championship. In the end though, Barr fell out of love with the scene, rather than the sport, and never harboured any illusions about a career in cycling. "I was decent enough. I could win races in Glasgow and still get some results in Scotland, but when I raced abroad, you realise that there are a lot of guys faster than you. I was level-headed enough not to have too many illusions on that score." Throughout his senior category years Barr had been training and studying as a civil engineer and ended up – of all places – in Ohio. Then Canada. Then New York and back to Beaconsfield in Buckingham in 2015 after a brief sojourn in Libya. "Yes, we've moved around a lot," laughs Barr, "but I've always ridden." Once a Wheeler...

While Barr was blazing his junior trail in 1986, schoolboy Stefan Collins was a real prospect on the track with Andrew Alexander making good progress on the roads too. True, Jamie McGahan had left to join the Greenock Road Club, but he had won the Scottish Health Race in 1983 and the Wheelers could still bask in *some* of his reflected glory.

With the rise in televised cycling on terrestrial TV and the arrival (in every sport) of various levels of sponsorship throughout the 1980s, it hadn't been that much of a shock when the Trustee Savings Bank (TSB) announced it was to sponsor the club for three years starting in 1987. Up to that point, cycling clubs had tended to snag support from local bike shops – thus the Johnstone Wheelers long association with Dooley's cycles – either officially or by way of discounts to members.

The arrival of non-cycling sponsors was a sign of things to come as new clubs simply named themselves after their sponsor. These new 'clubs' were more often that not essentially race teams, riders were invited to join, hand-picked and offered a level of financial support not possible with more traditional clubs. Arguably here we see the beginning of the end of cycling club culture – or at least a significant contributing factor.

Cycling clubs had been open to all, all levels of interest and ability, your club would welcome you from cradle to grave. You could join as a clueless youth, be taught the rules of the road by someone who had been riding for 40 years and learn the ropes – and the strands of that rope would include everything from gluing tubulars on to selecting the right wood for the drum-up fire, to wheeling about in the chain gang and honing race skills on club runs and 'habbles' for the 30 mph speed limit sign at village and town boundaries. It was no more complicated than that. Where was the room for those hands-on skills to be passed on in modern 'race team' structures and approaches? We digress, again.

Inevitably, the Wheelers club jersey had to change to accommodate the TSB logo, a move that was not universally approved, particularly by traditionalists who argued that you couldn't beat the classic, minimalist design that had been the Wheelers uniform for 60 years.

In fact it was the then chairman and club stalwart Eric Cruikshank who had been mainly responsible for attracting TSB funds to the club. The sums involved weren't astronomical, though they were in keeping with the time and amounted to a healthy injection of support. There was an initial £3,000 followed by two other payments of £1,500 in succeeding seasons – but it did allow some subsidy of riders and equipment between 1987 and 1989. (As a rough comparison, allowing for inflation and currency changes, £3,000 in 1987 was about £7,500 in 2022).

The arrival of TSB bank sponsorship also coincided with the arrival of some new senior talent, all active road racers. This may not have been a coincidence. Russell Scott and Steven Wylie jumped ship from the booming Glenmarnock Wheelers, Stevie Russell from East Kilbride Wheelers while John Sharples arrived from the Law Wheelers looking for a cool jersey and a club that was more active in road racing. Sharples, from Newmains near Wishaw, had raced since he was a junior "But all the clubs in central Scotland seemed to be more interested in time trials, I was looking for a road racing club and the original jersey design was cool!" recalls Sharples, "plus they had that Robert Millar connection." The performances of Hassan and Neil MacLeod, both pushing for international selection on the road, had also helped boost the profile of the club as a road racing outfit. The pair scored silver and bronze in the 1988 Scottish national road race, with MacLeod claiming a silver at the national hill climb championship that year too. For his part, Hassan also won the David Bell Memorial race. Young Russell was runner-up in the national junior road race too, with another youthful recruit Bruce Scott showing promise.

The arrival of TSB meant that, whatever their motivation, fresh blood had trickled in to the club. Stevie Russell (still racing in 2011!) had defected from the East Kilbride Wheelers and would go on to win the Scottish junior road race title in a Glasgow Wheelers jersey in 1989.

For Russell – now a bike shop owner at EK OK Bikes – the Wheelers were a club where an ambitious young rider could measure himself against some strong Scottish talent. "I joined as a junior in

1987 and I had ridden with the East Kilbride Wheelers since 1983. I went to the Wheelers because there were guys there like Russell Scot, Neil MacLeod, Davie Hassan, Gordon Plenderleith, Gordon Barr, Bruce Scott and if you won the club hill-climb championship you know you had beaten some good guys!" recalled Russell. Russell was living in East Kilbride at the time he joined and would ride from his home out to the club rides, do long days to the north of the city then ride home. "I used to have to stop in Rutherglen and get a can of Coke and a Boost bar, sit on the pavement and eat it just to make sure I could get up the East Kilbride road. But I'd usually ridden more than 100 miles by the time I made it home." Ah, tell that to kids today, etc...

Russell was not alone in bringing down the average age of the membership in this period though, with Stefan Collins having signed up in 1984. In fact Collins lived close to Lomond Roads CC clubroom, but confessed the colour scheme of the jersey put him off, Considering it was brown and yellow at the time, you can understand his reluctance to join the venerable west side outfit. "I had watched the Tour on telly and then went into Glasgow to see the Kellogg's city centre criteriums, I was a big fan of Phil Anderson. Actually I went up to Phil after the finish and, being a cheeky 13-year-old I asked if I could have his Peugeot cap. Well, he was handing it to me and some old guy snatched it first. Turns out the guy who grabbed it was Jimmy Marshall, who would end up as my first mentor!" Having dodged the Lomond Roads, Collins' first club would be the Glasgow United where, as a schoolboy, he took part in the epic club runs of the era, heading north to Comrie, Braco and Crieff. "I was on a Raleigh Arena with no toe clips and training shoes and – funnily enough – struggling on climbs. But I was OK in sprints, even then." It was at the United that Collins started racing as a schoolboy in 1983-84 with his team mate Liam Hassan, younger brother of Davie who was, at that point, rising through the ranks as a Glasgow Wheeler. Noting his turn of speed in a gallop, Collins was encouraged to try his hand at track racing and, specifically, sprinting and schoolboy Collins found himself at Westhorn track where Tommy Banks was organising the track league. A switch to the Wheelers was inevitable.

Schoolboy track racing often involved using road bikes still equipped with gears, brakes and road tyres and wheels but Collins was keen to do it properly. "I built up my track bike from bits and pieces, it was like something out of 'Breaking Away' really," laughs Collins now. "I was getting dropped in road races and crits around Kings Park and Bellahouston, but when it came to track racing – match sprints – that was a revelation to me, that was something I could do."

It had been several seasons since a Glasgow Wheelers skinsuit had been seen on the wooden boards going quite as fast as Collins and, ironically, it was the man now organising, Tommy Banks, who had filled that role.

From schoolboy to junior and senior, as an engineering student in pre-Lottery funding days, to the years when Edinburgh's open air Meadowbank track was the best facility in Scotland, these were not the easiest of times to be a Scottish-based track rider. Airdrie rider Stewart Brydon and Inverness' Eddie Alexander were the kingpins of Scottish sprinting at the time and Collins recalls that they were operating at a different level. In fact Alexander would go on to finish fourth in the 1988 Seoul Olympics behind Lutz Hesslich of East Germany and Nikolai Kovche with Alexander losing out to Australian Gary Neiwand in the bronze medal ride-off. Knowing what we know now about East German and USSR state-wide doping regimes, it looks like Eddie was unlucky, to say the least.

But we're straying off topic, the point being that Scotland was already producing world-class sprinters and Collins was in good company. In fact, the next generation of Scottish sprinters, Craig Maclean and Chris Hoy, were the new young duo that Collins would – literally – be rubbing shoulders with.

Curiously, Collins doesn't recall that there was much coaching input from Tommy Banks who, lest we forget, represented Scotland in the match sprint at the 1970 Commonwealth Games. Rather, Collins remembers advice from Jimmy Dorward. "He had me going around the (Cadder) graveyard, doing efforts that were about three minutes long. I remember I did the first one, flat-out, and Jimmy told me I had done really well, the time was terrific and now I should go and do the next one. I kinda looked at him, shocked. As far as I was concerned, that was my effort and I'd need a while before I attempted another!" Collins laughs at the memory, but in a pre-internet age, coaching manuals and advice – particularly for track sprinters – were thin on the ground. "I remember years later, when I was training with Eddie Alexander and Stewart Brydon, we were discussing training. Eddie was down in Gloucester by then and he was asking what riding I did. I told him most of my training was done in the gym and that I didn't ride during the week, I went to uni and that was about it. He was shocked and told me I should be riding into uni, pedalling at a high cadence and doing the odd effort, as well as the gym work. It seems obvious now, but at the time, I just didn't know."

Flirting with selection for the Scottish Commonwealth Games teams, Collins suggests that membership of the City of Edinburgh Road Club would probably have been a good 'career' move and, although Collins would ride as a 'second claim' member for other clubs and teams when the new three-rider 'Olympic sprint' (aka team sprint) was introduced to the track programme in 1995, Collins always maintained his Wheelers membership.

By the early 1990s, mountain biking arrived to distract the jaded and tempt those new to cycling away from road bikes. Increasingly crowded roads and the appeal of hills were only part of the 'crisis' in competitive cycling in Scotland. After the retirement of Millar in 1995 following the disintegration of his Le Groupement squad, there was no longer a comparable character to sell the sport to armchair Scottish sports fans.

Once again, the struggles of the Wheelers, as well as other clubs and race organisers were mirrored throughout Scotland. The membership of the SCU, based in a Portacabin next to Meadowbank stadium in the 1990s, was around 1,800. Of that, only around 800 had a racing licence which enabled the holder to take part in both time trials and road races. An SCU membership was all that you needed to race in open time trials though. When comparing with today's statistics it's worth noting that at this point there was no registration of youth categories and under-12 riders didn't register at all – in many senses! In 2022 those same boys and girls had licences which accounted for no fewer than 600 data points and, of course, mountain bike racers, now welcome inside British Cycling/Scottish Cycling, were living 'outside the law' as it were, uncounted and unregistered by the Federation in the early 1990s too.

The active road racing memberships of the Wheelers had already begun to dip by the mid-1990s, so much so that the trophy for club road champion – awarded to the rider who had scored the most points in road racing in a season, was barely contested. "I think it was in 1993," recalls Neil MacLeod, "I won the club road race champion trophy because I had finished sixth in one race. I mean, OK, it was a decent race, a Grand Prix event, but it was one race." And that one sixth place made MacLeod the 1993 club road race champion, but then in 1994 there had only been five SCU race licence holders at the club, out of a total membership of 48 – and seven of them were honorary members. The secretary that season, Joe Patterson noted, "I've seen a number of changes at the club, but during my time we have had riders who have reached the very top both nationally and internationally and it is very sad to say that we do not have one single member at junior or juvenile level." It was a portent of things to come.

If the Wheelers were no longer making headlines domestically in road racing, then there was still Graeme Obree to keep the club's name in the time trial headlines. Having said that, Obree's track and time trial exploits, as outrageous and newsworthy as they were, couldn't compete with the media coverage garnered by Robert Millar in the Tour de France (or the Tours of Spain or Italy, or the Criterium du *Dauphiné* Libere or Tour of Catalonia).

Obree was – albeit ephemerally – a Glasgow Wheeler, and the quixotic Ayrshire rider won the 1991 '25' title in a new record time while wearing a Glasgow Wheelers skinsuit adorned with Swiss clothing firm Assos logos. Billy Bilsland had negotiated a deal via the UK importer Phil Griffiths for discounted clothing which lasted two seasons. That arrangement lasted about as long as Obree's name on the club register.

Obree was a formidable rider against the clock and, on one occasion, warming up before a mid week '10' he was caught by another rider who Obree assumed was warming up. As they rode along and Obree chatted, he asked the rider, 'What time are you off?' to which the poor rider replied, 'This is me 'on'". The unavoidable truth is that in Scotland Obree's name will forever be associated with the Loudon Road Club and, latterly, the Wallacehill CC. Obree, a free-thinking maverick to his core, still offers his services and insights as a business speaker and consultant.

The mid-1990s were bleak years for the club, as many stalwarts found age catching up with them, which, allied to a lack of junior members and a dissipation of senior riders meant the active club roll was down to 25 members. The club nights moved to Crownpoint sports centre in the Gallowgate, but with fewer than 10 attendees most nights, the nights, too, were fading. The 1996 AGM noted that there were only five riders in the club with racing licences.

Towards the end of the 1990s the ageing profile of the Wheelers continued, with a drifting away of young talent from the club. There were a number of factors involved, and the Wheelers wasn't the only long-established club with a membership roll most of whom were eligible for a free bus pass.

The attraction of mountain biking in a country blessed by good public land access, countless miles of Forestry roads – and some actual mountains – played a part. The lack of high-profile continental or domestic professional role models to boost the sport's media profile also had an impact. Simultaneously, whatever young talent was about was being hoovered up by 'race teams' less invested in the old-fashioned club culture represented by the Glasgow Wheelers. All of which meant that numbers diminished as the new millennium loomed. Road cycling and club life was changing, again – because, well, how could it not? Nothing lasts forever.

In the words of one long-standing Wheeler, by the mid-1990s, "It was just a few old guys" and at one point, with so few riders racing, it was muttered that perhaps an amalgamation with the Glasgow Couriers would be a good idea. Happily, that nuclear option wasn't considered for too long, but it was an indication that the club was more or less on life-support.

At the end of the 1999 season, as the world braced itself to repel Millennium bugs, the end of season Scottish Cycling results booklet did not make for happy reading. There was not a single Glasgow

Wheeler named in the 61 riders who scored points in the seven-race Senior Grand Prix road race series. What about the Development road series? 64 riders were named as points scorers, but again there were no Wheelers.

Things were marginally better in the Veterans road race series with the indefatigable Tommy Banks and Bob Taylor scoring points in categories C and D (for racers over 60) but there were no women riders listed anywhere. How about in open time trials? The Wheelers merited one lonely mention – the resilient Jimmy Parker in the 60-plus category. The vital signs were not good and the Wheelers were leaving the 20th century heading for obsolescence.

8

THE MILLENNIUM BLUES

AS SCOTLAND FOUND its feet in the new millennium, things appeared to be picking up for the Glasgow Wheelers, relatively speaking. The bare fact was that given how the membership had shrunk, both in terms of numbers and geriatric muscle wastage, any growth would have been welcome.

The dust was settling on the mountain bike versus road bike 'wars' and both tribes began to grasp that it wasn't a case of being 'either/or' and that, in the end, it was all just bike riding, regardless of how fat the tyres were. If you wanted to go fast you had to press down on the pedals, no matter what size your wheels were.

Chairman Billy Bilsland had managed to persuade long-standing member George Murray to become secretary and Murray's enthusiasm and energy injected much-needed momentum into the club. The membership increased and, better yet, there was some new, younger, blood. Among those youngsters who joined was Jamie Drever, originally from Edinburgh but, like many modern club members, a student at Glasgow University at the time. "I had started riding a bike just through watching the Tour on TV, started riding a bit, but eventually thought I should join a club." And the club he joined turned out to be the Glasgow Wheelers.

Drever dutifully turned up for his first club run on a soaking wet Sunday in February 2002 and, by his own account, got to Aberfoyle in bits. "I thought I was quite fit, I was 24 at the time, but I was *so* naive, I didn't have a clue. I was begging these 'old guys' just to leave me in Aberfoyle," Drever laughs at the memory. Welcome to the bonk…

Drever was well and truly bitten by the cycling bug and threw himself into training, racing and club life. As he was studying IT and computing at university, he decided to set up a website for the club as part of his Masters thesis which is why, in 2002, the club was endowed with an all-singing, all-dancing website, complete with a searchable database history.

The website survived for 15 years but a lack of input from the members and an over-reliance on Drever led to it being replaced by a much more stripped-down site. Much archive material – photos, race reports and history was taken down (albeit a lot of that content has found its way into this book!) and some still floats in cyberspace. Within two years Drever, now working at Clydesdale bank, was the club treasurer, a post he would occupy for almost a decade.

Drever quickly graduated from getting a kicking on club runs to racing, moving from time trials to road racing. "Really, at the time, there was almost nobody in the club racing and there were a couple of seasons when I was often the only Wheeler in road races, though there were many of the old guard still time trialling, including Jimmy Parker. At the time George (Murray) would give me a lift to race starts, he was a massive help and there were others who had been at the club a long time too who helped, like John and Johan Thayne, Bob Taylor and Eric Cruickshank. In fact Jimmy (Parker) and Peter Harley would often be there at time trials too, giving me advice. They were like Wheelers royalty! Peter always telling me to eat a tin of rice pudding before a '50' time trial!"

Slowly, Drever was joined by like-minded souls and, in the opening years of the millennium, a new crop of racers turned up. One of them, Nicky Docherty, was just 18 when he joined which had the instant effect of lowering the average age of the club, although, more seriously, Docherty raced well enough to make it to first category status. He and Drever were joined shortly afterwards by Stuart McManus (son of Ivy CC 1980s strongman Jim) who showed great promise in the under-23 category, signing up in 2007. This trio were coached by –

inevitably – Jimmy Dorward, though Jimmy's brutal interval sessions had moved from the now too-busy Cadder cemetery 'triangle' down to Campsie glen.

The presence at races of a new generation of racing Wheelers generated some interest and a higher profile for the club, slowly attracting new members. In any case, even if there were still no youth or junior members and only a few seniors racing, the club's older contingent continued to compete with some success in the various veterans and Masters categories. It seemed like there was something of a resurgence of interest in the road racing side.

There was a recognition inside the club that the talent pool was drying up fast and some efforts were made to hatch a youth development strategy. It was a sign that the club hadn't quite given up the ghost. Perhaps there was still potential to emulate some of the successes of the past?

As fears of the Millennium bug receded, some senior Wheelers continued to compete in road, track and time trials with varying levels of success. In 2006 Brian Carlisle won gold at the British Masters, and in 2007 Isobel Fletcher additionally won bronze and the unstoppable Tommy Banks was still racing on track too at the World Masters championships. Club members continued to break age-related records, the most prolific of that era being Bob Taylor. However, at junior and senior levels, racing participation was still low, in spite of efforts to maintain a presence in the west of Scotland. It was not an affliction that was either new or unique to the Glasgow Wheelers among long-established cycling clubs.

In fact, there were more and more reasons to *not* join a cycling club, any club. In the early years of the Millennium, the phenomenon of the 'Sportive' mass-participation ride was growing in popularity – a cycling road event that wasn't a race, but was certainly a challenge. Sportives were often treated as a type of 'race' – even if the number was zip-tied to your handlebars rather than safety-pinned on your back. Whatever competitive itch that riders had was easier to scratch in a Sportive than a road race.

If there were no youth or junior riders on road bikes any more, it was no doubt partly because 'the kids' were out riding mountain bikes, with parents happier to see their offspring as far from increasingly traffic-clogged roads as possible.

It might also be true that the lack of a clear geographical 'heart' to the club played a role in its difficulty in attracting new riders. For all that the Wheelers is, obviously, a Glasgow club, it's not clear which *part* of Glasgow its from. It sounds trivial, but when the Nightingale are from the north, the Lomond Roads from the west, the Glenmarnock from the south west, where is the Wheelers base? Newly formed clubs like the Glasgow Green CC and VC Glasgow South, make it obvious. New, inexperienced or curious riders from those locations know *precisely* which club is nearest to them.

Nevertheless, given the club's history, the Wheelers was still capable of attracting some younger talent. After all, not everyone could afford to go to a race team and a few were still attracted by a club with such a long and distinguished heritage. In 2004 a former marathon runner turned cyclist called David Lang joined the club from the Ivy CC and, one way or another, he was to have a significant impact.

Lang, then in his fifties, was an enthusiastic racer and keen to revitalise the racing profile of the club, an eager talent scout and a man with both ambition and energy. For the 2008 season Lang had helped attract riders and snag some sponsorship from Alpine Bikes and WL Gore. "The sponsorship was mostly clothing," explains Drever, "but as treasurer I was able to get Sports Match funding from Sport relief which gave sports clubs a cash grant as a percentage of the goods in kind offered by any sponsors. I also managed to get £500 every year from the Clydesdale Bank which was supporting 'sport in the community' programmes. I always made sure the Wheelers qualified." Over his tenure as club treasurer Drever managed to accumulate around £13,000 for the coffers, helping support more ambitious riders to race further afield. The equipment that the club had – turbo trainers, disc wheels and track kit – was also funded. This included underwriting a team to race in the P&O Tour of the North stage race in Northern Ireland in 2008, the first time a Wheelers road team had ventured that far in years.

In fact, the jaunt across the Irish sea wasn't the only sign of road racing life. Considering that in 2003 Drever was the sole Wheeler competing in the renowned five-day Tour of the North in Northern Ireland as part of a composite team of Glasgow riders, this was progress indeed. At this time no other 'trad' Scottish club was entering these events, only race teams, so the Wheelers were on the comeback trail.

Interest grew amongst other riders and attracted new racers too, in part due to the Committee's continued funding of young riders. The Tour of the North was a step up from domestic Scottish racing, with both UK home grown clubs, UK race teams and foreign development squads participating, so anyone signing up was showing a healthy level of commitment.

For the next seven years the Wheelers would send road racing teams to Easter stage races such as Tour of the Borders, the Tour Doonhame as well as repeated editions of Tour of the North. In fact in 2010 the Club was able to send a team to the Premier Calendar Tour Doonhame in Dumfries as well as packing another six-rider team off to the Tour of the North. For some Wheelers this would be the peak of their road racing experience, whilst for others (most notably Robbie Hassan and Michael Nicholson) it would represent a first foray into top tier action before progressing to continental competition.

The focus of the Easter races during these years would ensure significant Club involvement in road races in early spring as well as bonding the club's riders through these 'away' events. The enthusiasm of the riders proved infectious and invigorated the club, with long-standing members like Eric Cruickshank and Neil MacLeod as well as Fiona McManus helping with physiotherapy, advice, catering and transport. The Wheelers was – for a time – an active racing club again.

If George Murray, Lang and Drever were trying to jolt the Wheelers back into the racing groove, then chairman Bilsland was doing his bit too. Billy got his stopwatch out – and his bike shop van. "There were sessions between 2004 and 2006 when Billy would be coaching a number of us. We'd ride out to Dullatur, do an interval session then Billy would get in the van and we'd do a motorpacing session, a team time trial, behind the van," recalls Drever. The chairman was still a racer at heart.

From around 2006 onwards, Neil MacLeod began to get more involved. MacLeod had first joined the club in 1980 and, other than a dalliance with the Bradford Wheelers when he was studying physiotherapy in Leeds, MacLeod been a Wheeler most of his adult life. MacLeod ran circuit and flexibility sessions and roller nights then took over the Spring-Summer sufferfest interval sessions as the ageing Dorward bowed out. A small group of younger riders (Drever, Keith Smith, Graeme Neagle, Michael Nicholson) began to coalesce, a number of them students who had been riding in their home towns before decanting to study in Glasgow. In 2010 David Griffiths, a Glasgow university medical student emigree from Wales signed up, joining Nicholson, Smith and Neagle (who joined in 2008, leaving at the end of 2014). Grant Stevenson was also part of a growing nucleus of active road racers at the club, who all of whom posted decent results on the Scottish domestic scene.

Nicholson didn't tarry too long at the club, heading out to Belgium in 2011 for a couple of seasons to try his luck and see how far his talent would take him with the ASFRA team. Nicholson actually returned to Scotland in the hope of making the squad for the Commonwealth Games in 2014 but, in qualification for the individual pursuit, a lap-count and timing SNAFU ruined his (strong) chance. At which point, quite reasonably, Nicholson's enthusiasm faded.

Unsurprisingly, as is usually the case, when riders in a club start to show form and get results, others follow. In due course, racing doctor Jason Roberts arrived, as did Andrew Whitehall, son of one of Scotland's finest 1980s all-rounders, David. Between them, these riders raced at domestic level on road and track. In the 2014 David Bell memorial road race, a classic Scottish hilly race held around Girvan, there were three Wheelers in the top 10 – Whitehall, Roberts and Griffiths.

Roberts, from Leicester, had relocated to Glasgow, working as a surgeon, and had joined the Glasgow Nightingale. "I was just starting to race again after being out for about 12 years and Davie Lang approached me to suggest I joined the Wheelers," recalls Roberts. "he said he was getting a bit of a race team together. So Davie was recruiting a bunch of riders and the only one of the group I knew was Rab (Wardell). But Dave Smith joined around then too and he had had a couple of seasons in France, racing with the support of the Braveheart fund, so he was a strong rider. There was Kristoff Aksnes and Dougie Young too as well as Robbie Hassan. Robbie was the youngest and a real talent, he was the 'wunderkind' of the group," chuckles Roberts "but it was a great time, we had a really good group of riders racing at a decent level."

It wasn't just the Roberts-Griffith-Smith-Hassan group who were racing at this point. In addition to his administrative duties, Drever was somehow racing too. With Nicky Cronin (who joined in 2010), and Whitehall showing in the SuperSix series, Lang, now over 60, was still road racing in SuperSix B-series too. There were more than just one or two Wheelers road racing again, and they were competing strongly at national level. Things were looking up.

Any history with claims to credibility will have to confront some controversy somewhere and, of course, the Wheelers has had its moments. It has to be recorded that part of the reason for the influx of talent from around 2007 onwards was down to the efforts of Lang, who worked hard to bring in some sponsorship and drive to the club. It is fair to say that Lang's efforts were not universally greeted with enthusiasm from all inside the club. Lang's efforts to modernise the club, to transform it into more of a racing team, raised the eyebrows of those who felt this development was at the expense of the wider membership and aims of the club.

Underneath the enthusiasm for this road racing resurgence, disquiet at the speed of changes inside the club fomented. Following the influx of single-minded racers, some of the 'Old Guard' were not overly impressed with the level of commitment being shown to the club. The complaint levelled against the young guns was that they were happy to take whatever the club offered but not give anything back when it came to supporting it. The Wheelers organised four events per season, two road races and two time trials, all of which needed marshals and organisation. Where was the young team then?

Nevertheless, what was clear to all, what all were agreed on, was that the club was withering away. What was *less* clear was what to do about it. Should the Wheelers become a race team? Perhaps it should take the steps required to set up a youth team? Who knows how the club might have developed, but then, as ever, the benefit of hindsight is a wondrous thing,

However, for a brief period, these underlying issues could be ignored. In 2010 the club enjoyed its best senior men's road racing results in decades, delivered variously by Griffiths, Neagle, Roberts, Hassan and Whitehall. The late Rab Wardell and Dougie Young as well as Dave Smith pitched in with quality senior road race results too. 2010 was something of a millennial high for the club's racing contingent when it seemed the only competition to the powerful Scottish clothing sponsored Endura team came from the Wheelers.

It couldn't last and, inevitably, it didn't.

The factions and opinions inside the club turned out to be irreconcilable and a controversial disciplinary procedure which saw a member expelled resulted in much bad feeling. Broadly speaking, the 'new racers' sided with the aggrieved party. If some had been thinking of changing clubs and others had been unhappy at the club's 'new direction,' this incident proved to be an explosive spark.

Additionally, in the course of trying to secure sponsorship for the club, Lang reckoned it would be better to set up ProVision Racing as a stand-alone entity. At which point, a split was inevitable. Any prospect of the Glasgow Wheelers being stealthily transformed – perhaps the 'Glasgow Wheelers ProVision Race Team' vanished there and then. Consequently the Committee decided that Lang should leave the club at the end of 2014 on the basis that a member should not – and could not – encourage club members to join another club. Exit Davie Lang. By that point, given the disciplinary and appeals process, Lang's new team was already in operation and the core of racing Wheelers had already defected prior to Lang's own defenestration. There is some small irony here, if we recall that the origin of the Glasgow Wheelers came about when four riders from the Douglas CC fell out with the club and left to form the Wheelers. History, repeating.

There is an argument – and its much easier to have in hindsight – that the club missed an opportunity at this point. Wasn't there a way to incorporate a 'race team' within the club, to offer some incentives to dedicated and enthusiastic competitive riders? With youngsters siphoned off by youth teams and committed senior racers joining race squads (and invariably paying for that privilege), the Glasgow Wheelers could have – and perhaps should have – offered more at this juncture in its history.

The counter argument to that is that not many long-established Scottish clubs were supporting their riders as well financially – helping with race entry, accommodation and travel expenses. Even as a 'traditional' cycling club, the Wheelers did offer support to racing members. The Wheelers had worked hard to obtain funding to support active riders but ultimately couldn't compete with the deeper pockets and glamour of the 'trade' teams. Perhaps the Glasgow Wheelers had actually been punching above its weight for years? The wider context is that exactly like other sports clubs, the Wheelers was yet another old organisation bamboozled by the shift between 'traditional' and 'modern' cycling?

The situation was summed up – inadvertently, cruelly, neatly – by Robbie Hassan. After a promising first senior season in 2009, Hassan had left the Wheelers to ride for Endura Pedal Power in 2011, winning his opening race of the season in his new colours. Asked by the *Velo Veritas* website about the team change Hassan said, "It was a great move. It's a good bunch of guys who are all keen to race; and the team provides kit and financial help with racing expenses." Ouch. Was it a wrench to leave the Glasgow Wheelers? "No, this is an upward step and the club wishes me well." An 'upward step' indeed. Ouch again.

Given the ageing profile of the club, unkind souls – or perhaps those with a decidedly Glaswegian sense of humour – suggested that in the early years of the new millennium, the club should be renamed the Geriatric Wheelers. The fact was that the average age of the membership was nearer super-veteran than junior and, when it came to actually pinning on a number and racing, the Masters categories were the most active by far. The junior membership that had been dwindling for years finally dried up. At the time of writing – in 2023 – there were no junior members of the Wheelers and although there was never a massive junior grouping at any point in the club's history, this is a historic low, albeit its a state of affairs mimicked in almost all long-established Scottish cycling clubs. The landscape – sporting, economic and cultural – has changed and goes some way to explaining the youth drought.

If there are no youth or junior riders at the Wheelers, that is also partly down to the fact that a cycling club with young members now must have a child protection contact as well as a welfare 'officer' to deal with bullying and inclusion issues. Members working with under sixteens are required to sign up for police background checks (renewed every three years) too. Laudable as these measures are, it was never going to be easy to find volunteers eager to take on these significant responsibilities. To add some context, in 2006 the document 'Scottish Cycling child protection policy' had 67 pages, covering everything from the role of a club's child protection officer to "managing challenging behaviour" as well as offering a bibliography for further reading. The *entire* 1949 A5-sized SCU handbook contained a total of 32 pages.

Broadly speaking, the new requirements are down to the spread – in the early 2000s – of what might be termed 'sports governance.' In large part this new bloom of regulations and governance is down to money. Essentially, if a Scottish sports club receives financial aid or services from its governing body then, ultimately, that money can be traced back to government coffers via Sport Scotland.

If it turned out that taxpayers' money was being used by a woman-hating kiddie-fiddling bully in a cycling club – which did *not* have background checks and protocols in place – that would not make good tabloid headlines. That flippant summation is as far as we need to go in this history. Simply, if Scottish Cycling wants a slice of government money, it has to sign up to its governance and regulatory framework. Consequently, if a cycling club wants to affiliate to Scottish Cycling, it needs to sign up to those same duty of care rules too.

In 2023, if your cycling club is part of Scottish Cycling then the digital and regulatory challenges that the club secretary is required to negotiate are numerous and time consuming.

Idle speculation might lead you to wonder if, in the near future, 'old fashioned' cycling clubs will think it worthwhile to affiliate to Scottish (British) Cycling. Do such clubs really need to fill in forms and pay £100 affiliation fees and a further £68 to register each sponsor? After all, if your members are only interested in club runs to a cafe, time trialling, a couple of sportives and a reliability trial, you don't need a BC race licence or even membership of Scottish Cycling do you? The Glasgow Wheelers was up and racing more than 20 years before the Scottish Cyclists' Union existed, so one might reasonably – if treasonably – ask what the current incarnation of the Wheelers really needs with Scottish Cycling. Yet again, we digress, albeit for the final time.

Inescapably, we've come a long way from Pat McCabe helping out Jamie McGahan with that puncture on the Garscube road or John Storrie scooping up Robert Millar in the mid 1970s. Back then every club had an old guy – and sometimes he wasn't even *that* old – but he was always a guy, who acted as a recruiting sergeant and road captain. He was the one who led club runs, schooled the newcomers and knew where all the drum-up spots were. For the first 80 years of Scottish club cycling history, the only qualifications required for the job were experience and willing.

So, while new Glasgow Go-Ride 'youth' clubs were hoovering up keen kids, it's no surprise that the average age of the Wheelers rose, while the membership was on the wane. If few Wheelers were keen enough to jump through the hoops required to accommodate under sixteens, other clubs were.

Thus, any interested young riders and their parents gravitated towards the Clydesdale Colts or the Johnstone Wheelers junior team, the Johnstone Jets. There was the Glasgow Riderz too, formed in 2004 specifically to cater for the youth categories. These youth outfits were set-up with help through British Cycling's 'Go-Ride' programme and the waiting lists for youngsters is testimony to their popularity. Those in central Scotland have memberships of between 50 and 80 riders.

However, there are mutterings that Go-Ride clubs offer a cheap 'crèche' for some parents looking to offload the kids at the weekend. The meagre 'graduation' rate once youth riders enter junior categories suggests there might be some truth in that analysis. If there's a feeling that there are too many children being dumped on youth cycling clubs for babysitting, well, the difficulty of the sessions can always be cranked up a degree by the coach, to see who really *is* keen...

To appreciate how much those Under-12 and Youth category clubs might be being (ab)used as somewhere to deposit the kids on a Saturday morning, consider this. In 2022 there were no fewer than 725 licenced youth and under-12 riders on the books of Scottish Cycling. Sadly, that same year, data shows that there were only 150 male and female Juniors combined. From 725 schoolkids to a mere 150 Juniors – of which just 25 were girls – in the whole of Scotland. This is not to denigrate Scottish Cycling's efforts, merely to point out that when it comes to attracting and holding on to young riders, it's not easy in the modern era with its myriad distractions. Traditional cycling clubs who imagine that a Go-Ride set-up attached to the 'parent' club will guarantee a stream of keen and well-coached juniors, are likely to be disappointed.

For those eager youngsters who *do* go on to compete as juniors, there are 'race teams' waiting to snatch them up and offer bikes, clothing, coaching, transport and a race programme tailored to their sporting aspirations. The offer of such bounties comes at a price of course, but for those willing (and able) to invest two or three thousand pounds a season in racing, you can see the appeal.

Given that backdrop, what does the future hold for the Glasgow Wheelers as an active racing club? The least that can be said is that the club will continue for as long as there are riders who want to be part of the long and intermittently glorious history of the Glasgow Wheelers. Will the club ever be a formidable racing outfit again? The harsh truth is that modern developments conspire against such an eventuality. The Glasgow Wheelers, once a force in club racing, isn't a racing *team* and, in 2023, that is what would be required to generate a racing revival.

We shouldn't be downhearted. Scottish road racing might be bumping along, casting around for riders' entries in the same way it has done for decades, but cycling as a pastime and mode of transport has a higher profile than at any time in the past 40 years. Concerns over the nation's health, carbon emissions and sustainable transport have given cycling an important place in a crucial international debate. Such is cycling's profile now that it is no longer seen as the weird 'Do you shave your legs and wear Lycra?' fringe cult it once was.

One hundred years after the club's birth, cycling is a much more mainstream pursuit, though domestic racing is still a niche activity, at best. Every cycling club in the UK has benefited from ephemeral boosts in popularity generated by numerous Olympic successes since Beijing in 2008, even after the surge of enthusiasm and media coverage fades, newcomers introduced to 'the bike' stick with it.

Consider the massive boosts to cycling clubs offered by the arrival of Team Sky and Mark Cavendish's world road title in 2010, Sir Chris Hoy's velodrome heroics at the London 2012 Olympics and the successes of Bradley Wiggins' throughout that season, including Britain's first overall win at the Tour de France. Since 1997 there's been a new generation of Lottery-funded male and female British riders boosting cycling's public profile higher than it had ever been. True, despite those medals and rainbow jerseys, racing licence numbers hover around 10,000 souls in the UK, about the same number in the pre-Lottery 1990s but given the decline in participation in other sports we shouldn't be too despondent. Does anyone remember squash clubs? Golf? Or is your local golf course now a housing development?

Hot on the heels of the London 2012 Games came the 2014 Commonwealth Games in Glasgow. Those Games saw a potential boost for Scottish cycling – and Glasgow-based riders in particular – with the building of the Sir Chris Hoy velodrome in the east end of the city. Constructed as part of the successful bid to host the Commonwealth Games, Glasgow now had a world-class facility and a new headquarters for Scottish Cycling. Almost half a century after Meadowbank velodrome was – reluctantly – built for the Edinburgh Games in 1970, it was Glasgow's turn and, this time, for the first time, a Scottish velodrome had a roof. After four decades of Glasgow riders travelling east to take a chance on the Edinburgh weather at roofless Meadowbank, the boot was now on the other foot.

The Hoy velodrome has enabled Scotland to host world and European championships, Commonwealth Games and World Cups, but it hasn't led to a spike in domestic racing participation, albeit there's been a steady trickle of world-class trackies. Perhaps we've become blasé about the international performances of Katie

Archibald, Neah Evans, Jack Carlin, Luisa Steele, Lewis Stewart and the rest. Or maybe we expected too much? We built it, but they didn't come, as it were.

The stark truth is that the number of Scottish Cycling race licences has actually remained more or less the same since 2012, British cycling's *annus mirabilis*. As with the wider UK, the hoped-for legacies from international events and media coverage of Scottish stars has not provoked a lasting uptick in interest either. Overall, the Scottish domestic racing scene is no healthier now – in terms of participating numbers or events – than it was in the 1970s. Glasgow might now have a world class velodrome, but there were only four entrants for the 2022 Men's individual pursuit championship. In that year's Scottish track championship bunch title races there were often only 10 or 12 riders on the start sheet and no Madison event. That same year, the winter track league often saw 'A' and 'B' groups combined in endurance races and just 14 juniors contested the national junior road race title. Cycle sport is still fundamentally for cyclists and the hoped-for crossover into the sporting mainstream has stalled.

There's *still* reason to smile though, and, perhaps, still scope for expansion. While the racing history of the Wheelers over the first hundred years was heavily tilted towards male riders, the best international results in the new millennium came from a woman. In fact Neah Evans was the first ever Glasgow Wheeler (or even former Glasgow Wheeler) to win an Olympic medal. After Jackie 'Mulguy' Bone in 1936 and Billy Bilsland in 1970 were given Olympic blazers, it fell to Evans to convert British Olympic Games selection into metal. Evans got a ticket for the '2020' Tokyo Games and, riding as part of the women's team pursuit squad, came away with a silver medal when the Games were finally run in 2021.

Evans was originally from the frozen north east, near Turriff in Aberdeenshire, but ended up at Glasgow university studying to be a vet as a mature student. Although Evans had been a hill runner, an injury saw her switch to cycling in 2014, racing in the British University championships that season. After the Glasgow Commonwealth Games, Scottish Cycling had opened its doors to new riders, and Evans went along with another Glasgow Wheeler and university student Jess Lee. Lee, who would go on to race for Hong Kong as a track sprinter, introduced Evans to the joys of track racing and, after a brief dalliance with sprinting, discovered her true talent lay in endurance events. According to one eye-witness, Evans' early forays onto the boards in the Sir Chris Hoy velodrome were neither trouble nor crash-free, but she evidently had huge talent and even more determination.

Evans, whose dad had been a cyclist and whose mother had competed for Great Britain in the winter Olympics in Sarajevo in cross-country skiing, made speedy progress. Evans quickly found herself as part of the Scottish squad then made the team at the 2018 Commonwealth Games, having already been talent spotted by British Cycling in Manchester. At the Brisbane track on Australia's Gold Coast, Evans came back home with a silver medal in the scratch race and packed that beside a bronze medal she collected in the points race. Before she – or we – knew it Evans had packed her bags, headed to Manchester to join the British Cycling squad and continued her upward progress. Neah might only have been an active member of the Wheelers for two seasons, but the club did play a part in her development and Evans is now an honorary vice president.

Given that she won a rainbow jersey in the points race at the 2022 world track championships at St Quentin-en-Yvelines near Paris, this was the least the club could offer. This triumph came on the back of terrific performances on road and track at the 2022 Birmingham Commonwealth Games where she won a silver in the points race and bronze in the individual pursuit – not forgetting a terrific silver medal in the women's road race. Her 2022 British titles in the pursuit and points almost seem like a footnote, given such stellar international performances.

In fact Evans has a strong claim to being the first Glasgow Wheeler to win a world title on road or track. In the interests of accuracy, Graeme Obree's individual pursuit titles in 1993 and 1995 should also be noted but, given Obree was already a well-established rider during his one-season sojourn with the club, it could safely be argued that the Wheelers had more influence on Neah's early development than it ever did on Graeme's!

If, overall, there is an elegiac tone to this final chapter it's because clearly something *has* been lost from Scottish cycling culture. The club nights, the youth hostel weekends on 'car free' roads and the drum-ups, the passing on of club folklore, even, to some extent, the skills required to ride in bunch – are ebbing away.

It's not all doom and gloom though. The youngsters being coached in Glasgow's Go-Ride clubs are learning the sport in the best conditions possible, often instructed by those who were schooled the old-fashioned way in the 1980s, notably Neil MacLeod. On the other hand, those who parachute into the sport as thirty-something ex-golfers and turbo-trained thoroughbreds (unsurprisingly) know little of club culture, etiquette or how to ride in an echelon. The traditions, times and organisations where such skills were imbued have all but vanished.

For decades the Rothesay cycling weekend was massive, a 'must do' for Glasgow riders, part competition, part end-of-season gathering of the cycling clans. Equally, the Isle of Man International bike week in May always saw a large Scottish contingent, mixing it with the best in Britain in a festival of non-stop racing. Part holiday, part racing festival, this cycling destination also withered away in the final years of the last millennium. The Isle of Man was no longer a cycling holiday destination, replaced by the Spanish Costas and Mallorca once Easyjet flights became available from 1996 onwards. The delights of stormy ferry trip to rain-lashed Peel lost their appeal when you could fly off to sunny Spain. Truly, a case of *España por favor.*

The friendships, rivalries and networks made at the Isle of Man and Rothesay have gone, replaced by other forms of connection and communication. The modern rider has GoPro video clips posted on social media platforms, WhatsApp groups, Strava clubs, virtual races on Zwift, phone camera selfies and instant online race results. It's *still* cycling – but its different.

The technology isn't the only thing that has changed of course. While we mourn the struggles of traditional road racing to find a place on Scotland's roads, other forms of racing and riding have been revived. Back in the 1920s 'Rough Stuff' enthusiasts would combine touring and mountain biking on machinery and gears that look totally unsuited to the pursuit. Today, with carbon frame sets and some smart gearing all mated to revamped brake and wheel technologies, this is now called 'gravel' riding.

In 2023, the UCI is running a world championship Gravel race, as well as a Europe-wide gravel race series, while mass-participation gravel events attract thousands of entrants. Cycle racing might be being pushed off the roads, but other options are available and enthusiastically taken up. We can recall that in the late 1980s cross-country mountain biking was greeted as the future of cycling, to the point at which road bikes gathered dust in bike shops all over the country. Mountain biking was *the* future. That turned out not to be the case and, in due course, everyone settled down and a new balance between these branches of cycle sport was achieved.

Perhaps gravel riding does have a wider appeal and application than mountain biking though. Given the increasingly hostile road environment, riding on gravel on a light, fast modified road bike holds an appeal that mountain biking never did.

Happily, there are Glasgow Wheelers taking part in these – and similar – events, so take a bow Robbie Martin and Neil Griffiths for keeping the competitive flame alive in what still seems to be a growing branch of cycle sport.

As the years pass, members age and ride off to the big drum-up in the sky, we can't pretend that there will be a return to the glory days of Jackie Bone, Jimmy Brinkins, Alex Hendry, Billy Bilsland and Robert Millar – the world and cycling have both changed too much for that to be a realistic possibility.

So, despite the best efforts of stalwarts and enthusiasts, the culture of the club has gone, shifted online to photo-caption nostalgia on Facebook. When riders can train indoors in virtual races with power meters and heart rate monitors – allied to zero chance of crashing on ice or being wiped out by a car – the attraction of a bone-chilling club ride on a winter's day understandably loses some of its appeal.

When private gym memberships – home gyms even – and reams of free cycling news on the internet are available, where is the incentive to attend a club night? Who still feels the need to share a barbell and pass around a dog-eared copy of *Cycling Weekly* for results and gossip from the previous weekend's races?

These days are over, though we can regret their passing along with the camaraderie, culture and solidarity they helped generate. Nevertheless, for as long as there are riders willing to push on the pedals and riders who want to be associated with a fine tradition and history, we can be confident that there are still years of Glasgow Wheelers history yet to be written.

Thanks and acknowledgments

THERE ARE MANY helpers to thank, though most have their names in the text! Tommy Banks, Billy Bilsland, Jamie Drever, Kath McCormack, Donald Sharp, John, Johan and Iain Thayne, Sarah Hendry as well as Pippa York all merit particular thanks for stories, time and documents. Sandra Pryde did the proof reading and 'Queen of Fonts, Shapes and Colours' Katie Pryde designed the cover. Where would I be without them?

Beyond that, dear god, where to start? Alphabetically, probably. So, thanks to Gordon Barr, Neil Bilsland, Graeme Brown, Stef Collins, Brian Cookson, Alan Fairweather, Alfie Fairweather, Andy Ferry, William Fotheringham, Gordon Goldie, Jason Griffiths, Mike Lawson, Neil MacLeod, Jamie McGahan, George Miller, Billy Munro, Stevie Russell, Alistair Rutherford, Tom Scott, John Sharples, Brian Smith, Chris Thomson, Harry Tweed, Velo Veritas, David Whitehall.

All errors and biases are mine.

Index

A
Aberfoyle 5, 8, 85, 105, 114-116, 139, 140
ACBB 106, 107, 128
AG2R 108
Aksnes, Kristoff 145
Alexander, Andrew 131
Alexander, Eddie 125, 134, 135
Alexandra Palace 24
Alpine Bikes 142
Anderson, Phil 106, 107, 120, 133
Annable, Brian 101
Archibald, Katie 151
Attlee, Clement 32, 47
Ayr Roads CC 61

B
Bagnères-de-Luchon 103
Banks, Tommy 92, 96, 97, 99, 100, 123, 133, 134, 138, 141, 157
Barr, Gordon 129, 133, 157
Bartali, Gino 127
Baxter, Jim 95
BBAR 17, 18
BBC 1, 24
BC 8, 54, 149
BCF (British Cycling Federation) 54, 58, 59, 64, 85, 100
Bellahouston Park 21, 117
Bennett, Michael 129
Berlin 23, 52, 89
Best All-Rounder 17, 23, 87, 118, 125, 128, 130
Bettinson, John 63, 89
Bicycle 2-4, 6, 10, 18, 19, 21, 53, 120
Bicycle Action 120
Bilsland, Alec 13
Bilsland, Billy 59, 62, 72, 74, 86, 91, 93, 103-105, 117, 118, 122, 123, 136, 139, 152, 155, 157
Bilsland, Ian 93, 97, 99
Bilsland, Neil 157
BLRC 19-21, 28-32, 40-47, 52-54, 104, 111
BMX 119
Boddy, Neil 126
Bone, Jackie 22, 23, 34, 35, 63, 66, 89, 102, 155
Boyd, Hughie 82
Braveheart 145
Brierley, Grace 51
Brierley, John 52, 55
Brinkins, Jimmy 13, 25, 26, 31, 35-37, 46, 60, 123, 155
British Best All-Rounder 17
British Broadcasting Corporation 1
British Cycling Federation 53, 54, 58, 99
British Cycling Union 17
British League of Racing Cyclists (BLRC) 18, 19, 21, 28, 40, 41
British Olympic Association 125
Brown, Jimmy 69
Brydon, Stewart 134, 135
BSA 6, 101, 102
Buckley, Peter 88, 130
Burton, Beryl 50

C
Cadder 60, 113, 124, 134, 141
Calder, Alex 45, 71, 73, 82, 85, 86
Calder, Jimmy 71
Cambuslang CC 36
Campagnolo 55, 64, 65, 101, 102
Campbell, Arthur 29-31, 40-42, 44, 46, 54, 55, 64-66, 69, 75, 82, 83, 97-99, 105, 107, 121, 122, 125, 127
Campbell, Isla 64
Campbell, Rab 73, 85
Campsies 37
Carlin, Jack 152
Carter, Neil 10
Cassels, Hugh 7, 12, 13
Catalunya 125

Chanel Four 120
Chryston Wheelers 8, 15, 30, 31, 40, 42, 43, 120
City of Edinburgh Road Club 101, 135
Clermont Ferrand 91
Clutha Ladies CC 50
Clydesdale Colts 149
Coll, Martin 121
Collins, Stefan 131, 133
Columbus 103
Commonwealth Games 26, 57, 60, 79, 88, 93, 96-100, 106, 121, 125, 134, 135, 144, 151-153
Conconi, Francesco 124, 125
Connor, Jackie 115, 122
Cook, Tom 32
Coventry CC. 36, 63
Cowal Games 20
Crawford, Sandy 96
Crawford, Tommy 7, 12, 13
Cronin, Nicky 145
Crow Road 30, 37, 60, 128
Crownpoint 137
Cruickshank, Eric 140, 143
CSM Puteaux 90, 92, 94
CTC 39, 59
Cumberworth, Maurice 63, 89
Cycling Weekly 13, 17, 28, 92, 94, 127, 155, 156
Cyclists Touring Club 39, 59

D

Daily Express 46, 82
Dale, Adam 20
Dales Cycles 20
Danguillaume, Jean-Pierre 90, 91
Dauphiné Libere 136
David Bell Memorial 61, 132, 144
Dawes 6
Del Vecchio, Val 7, 12, 13
Delgado, Pedro 76
Dewar, Rab 83, 84
Dick, Tommy 30, 31
Docherty, Nicky 140

Dorward, Jimmy 51, 52, 59, 62, 85, 87, 89, 93, 97, 112, 122, 129, 134, 140, 141
Douglas CC 8, 146
Drever, Jamie 139, 140, 142-145, 157
Drummond Trophy 61, 83, 96, 130
Drummond, Norrie 83
Dukes Pass 71, 73, 85, 88
Duncan, John 117, 122, 123
Dundee Thistle CC 9
Dunlop 4, 6, 50
Dunlop, William Boyd 4
Dunoon 20, 27, 45, 112
Duntocher-Dunoon 20, 21

E

Earley, Martin 120
East Kilbride 83, 84, 117, 132, 133
East Kilbride Wheelers 84, 132, 133
Edinburgh Road Club 35, 101, 135
Edwards, George 29-31, 40-43, 69
Empire Games 56
Equipe 90
Escalon, Claude 128
Evans, Ken 92
Evans, Neah 79, 152
Evening Times 2, 82

F

Facebook 155
Fairweather, Alan 118, 121, 157
Fairweather, Alfie 55, 58, 83, 96, 120, 129, 157
Fancourt, Jack 25, 66
Ferry, Andy 123-125, 154, 157
Flanders 12, 83, 87, 116
Flanders Moss 116
Fletcher, Isobel 141
Flying Scot 6, 35, 38, 55, 102, 103, 111, 112
Fraser, Colin 110, 112
Fullarton Wheelers 121, 122

G

Gallacher, Joe 35
Gardner, Ian 73, 85
Gentleman, Finlay 77

Gilbertfield Wheelers 36, 50
Gilchrist, Sandy 60, 98, 105, 106
Giro d'Italia 12
Girvan 86, 144
Glasgow Clarion 46, 97
Glasgow Commonwealth Games 152
Glasgow Corporation Transport CC 8
Glasgow Couriers 137
Glasgow Eastern CC 15
Glasgow Green CC 142
Glasgow Herald 20, 21
Glasgow Ivy 15
Glasgow Merchants CC 8
Glasgow Nightingale 15, 129, 144
Glasgow Riderz 149
Glasgow Road Club 58
Glasgow Suburban CC 8
Glasgow Transport CC 50
Glasgow United 22, 23, 52, 133
Glasgow United CC 22
Glasgow University 139, 144, 152
Glasgow Wheelers i, iii, ix, x, 1, 5, 7, 10-13, 15, 21, 25, 28-31, 33, 35, 37-41, 44-46, 48, 50-53, 60, 61, 66, 83-85, 93, 96, 97, 104, 105, 107, 114, 115, 120-123, 125, 132, 134, 136, 137, 139, 141, 146, 147, 149, 150, 155, 156
Glasgow-Dunoon 26, 87
Glass, John 70
Glenmarnock Wheelers 82, 92, 103, 132
Gordon, Sandy 60, 86, 87, 93, 96-98
Grangemouth Cycling Club 100
Greenock Road Club 131
Griffiths, David 144
Griffiths, Jason 157
Griffiths, Neil 155

H

Hamilton, Dougie 70, 71
Hannah, Dave 57
Hardie, Alex 36
Harley, Peter 120, 129, 140
Hassan, David 128
Hassan, Liam 133
Hassan, Robbie 143, 145, 147
Heatherbell Ladies CC 9
Hendry, Alex 26, 29, 30, 35, 37, 41-45, 66, 69, 155
Hendry, Jim 103
Herety, John 120
Hesslich, Lutz 134
Hetchins 102, 112
Hezard, Yves 91
Hinault, Bernard 64
Holland, Charles 23
Hoy, Sir Chris 82, 134, 151, 153
Hutchison, Alec 70

I

Inches, Billy 128
Inches, Willie 84
International Olympic Committee (IOC) 54, 108, 126
Isle of Man 23-25, 58, 66, 88, 106, 154
Ivy CC 61, 97, 140, 142

J

John Brown Shipyard 61
Johnstone Jets 149
Johnstone Wheelers 15, 51, 57, 85, 131, 149
Jolly, Brian 89
Jones, Rita 51

K

Kellogg's 77, 120, 121, 133
Kelly, Sean 98, 120

L

Lafferty, Frank 122
Laidlaw, Kenny 87
Laing, Maurice 114
Lake of Mentieth 123
Lang, David 142
Lavenu, Vincent 108
Law Wheelers 15, 132
Lawson, Mike 60, 77, 118, 121, 129, 157
Lawson, Stewart 122

Leblanc, Jean-Marie 94
Lemond, Greg 120
Logan, Alex 71, 82
Lomond Roads CC 15, 133
London Olympics 120
Los Angeles Games 126
Loudon Road Club 137

M

Macauley, Bob 73, 85
Maclean, Craig 134
MacLeod, Neil 78, 118, 132, 133, 136, 143, 144, 154, 157
Malcolm, Andy 7, 12, 13
Manx International 23, 89
Marsgate 73, 84
Marshall, Jimmy 133
Martin, Robbie 155
Marx, Karl 10
Maryhill Wheelers 92
McCabe, Pat 13, 29, 30, 34, 67, 111, 116, 123, 149
McCann, Joe 123
McDaid, Gerry 54, 64
McGahan, Jamie 60, 61, 96, 110, 111, 114, 123, 128, 131, 149, 157
McGhee, Andy 62
McGowan, Ashby 123
McGowan, Ashley 104
McGuire, Hughie 83
McLatchie, Sammy 110, 122
McLaughlin, Mick 116
McLeod, Rab 114
McMahon, Andy 31
McManus, Fiona 143
McManus, Stuart 140
McQuaid, Pat 98
Meadowbank 99, 101, 134, 135, 151
Mercian 103
Merckx, Eddy 89, 90, 109, 127
Merite Velo 90
Messenger, Chas 42
Mexico City 63, 89
Milan-San Remo 12
Milk Race 56, 62, 83, 88
Millar, Davie 120

Millar, Robert 60, 64, 76, 97, 103, 104, 110, 111, 113, 114, 117-119, 122, 123, 132, 136, 149, 155
Miller, George 54, 157
Milne, Willie 25, 35
Ministry of War Transport 32
Montgomery, Stewart 30, 41, 42, 44, 69
Morrison, Donald 13, 25, 26, 34, 35, 66
Munro, Billy 93, 96, 157
Murray, George 139, 140, 143

N

National Cyclists Union 2, 16, 31, 46
National Lottery 120
National Service 27, 37, 39, 40, 83
NCU 16-21, 26-29, 31, 32, 42-44, 46, 47, 52-54
Neagle, Graeme 144
Nicholson, Michael 143, 144

O

Obree, Graeme 27, 136, 137, 153
OC Plastics 115, 126
Olympic Games 23, 64, 89, 152
Omini, Agostino 127
Opperman, Hubert 24

P

Painter, Bill 58
Paris-Dreux 90, 92
Paris-Ezy 90
Paris-Mantes 90
Paris-Roubaix 12, 40
Paris-Tours 91
Park, Ronnie 87
Parker, Jimmy 70, 138, 140
Patterson, Joe 31, 35, 46, 68, 82, 126, 136
Peace Race 52, 53, 62, 64, 72, 75, 91
Peiper, Allan 107, 120
Pelissier, Henri 11
Penny Farthing 4
Pettigrew, John 31
Peugeot 64, 76, 91, 94, 103, 106-109, 117, 128, 133

Plenderleith, Gordon 133
Post, Peter 109
Potter, Jackie 13, 35, 110
Potter, Tommy 13, 20

R
Raleigh 6, 9, 55, 109, 133
Ramblers Association 9
Rangers FC 45, 95
Rankin, Avril 50
Rappoert Tour 98
Rattray, David 6, 13, 35, 38, 40, 102, 103, 110
Regent CC 15, 98, 115
Reith, John 1
Reynolds 38, 102, 103
Ritchie, John 87
Road Racing Council 16
Road Time Trials Council 16, 28, 47
Roberts, Jason 144
Roche, Stephen 120
Rollinson, Dave 63, 89
Rosslyn CC 9
Rourke, Brian 58
Royal Albert CC 15
RRC 16, 30
RRTC 28
RTTC 16, 18, 28, 47, 53
Russell, Stevie 130, 132, 157
Rutherglen Nomads CC 15

S
SACA 16, 20, 21, 46
Sam Robinson Memorial 61, 86
SARA 5, 16
Scally, Ernie 86, 87
Scot, Russell 133
Scotia CC 60, 61, 89, 113
Scott, Bruce 130, 132, 133
Scottish Amateur Cycling Association 16, 46
Scottish Amateur Racing Association 5, 16
Scottish Best All-Rounder 23, 130
Scottish Cyclists Union 2, 32, 46, 54, 61, 64, 81, 96, 99, 125, 149
Scottish Daily Express 82
Scottish Daily Record 27
Scottish Empire Exhibition 21
Scottish Health Race 131
Scottish Mountaineering Club 9
Scottish Youth Hostel Association 39
Seoul Olympics 134
Sharples, John 132, 157
Sheridan, Eileen 50
Simpson, Tommy 64, 92
Smith, Brian 127, 128, 157
Smith, John 90
Smith, Keith 144
Sport Scotland 148
Sportive 141
St Christopher 8, 36, 84
Stallard, Percy 20, 24, 28, 41, 42, 53
Stamperland Wheelers 50
Starley, John Kemp 6
Steel, Ian 52, 55
Steele, Luisa 152
Stella Maris 8
Stewart, John 13, 31, 35
Stirling University 1
Storrie, John 43, 104, 149
Strava 154
SYHA 39

T
T. T. 44
Tagg, Willie 13
Taylor, Bob 138, 140, 141
Taylor, Jack 116
Team Sky 120, 151
Team TSB 125
Thayne, Iain 118, 121, 157
Thayne, Johan 73, 85, 129, 140
Thayne, John 3, 13, 30, 34, 46, 51, 70, 71, 82, 93, 117
Thayne, Robert 45, 71, 116
Thayne, Willie 31, 38
The Bicyclist 19
Thevenet, Bernard 91
Thomson, Chris 127, 157
Thomson, Hector 83
Thomson, Ian 57, 61, 83, 87, 97, 113
Tokyo Games 152

Tour de France	11, 12, 24, 25, 38, 64, 87, 89, 91, 94, 103, 120, 121, 136, 151
Tour Doonhame	143
Tour of Austria	88, 98
Tour of Britain	41, 43, 44, 46, 52, 53, 55, 56, 69, 70, 77, 82, 113
Tour of Catalonia	136
Tour of East Germany	56
Tour of Flanders	12
Tour of Lombardy	12, 92
Tour of Scotland	21, 62, 82, 87, 91, 106
Tour of Slovakia	74
Tour of Spain	76
Trustee Savings Bank	125, 131
TSB	125, 126, 131, 132
TT	23, 117
Turnbull, Tommy	10

U

Union Cycliste Internationale (UCI)	26, 29, 30, 32, 43, 47, 53, 54, 64, 65, 75, 82, 89, 98-100, 108, 115, 126, 127, 155
USSR	115, 134

V

VC Glasgow South	142
VC Stella	57, 86, 87, 97
Velo Veritas	98, 117, 147, 157
Verbruggen, Hein	108
Veteran Time Trial Association	35
Vogt, R. A.	4, 5

W

Wadley, Jock	19
Wallace, Jimmy	13, 34
Wardell, Rab	144-146
Warsaw-Berlin-Prague	52
Webb, Ron	101
West, Les	89, 90
Westcott CC	36
Whitehall, Andrew	124, 144-146, 157
Whitehall, David	124, 157
Wiggins, Bradley	120, 151

Wright, John	117
Wylie, Steven	132

Y

Yates, Sean	120
York, Philippa	103, 106
Young, Dougie	145, 146

Z

Zoetemelk, Joop	89, 91
Zwift	154

WS - #0118 - 130824 - C4 - 216/140/10 - PB - 9781915972163 - Matt Lamination